SMALL *Oxford* BOOKS

BOATING

Also by Christopher Dodd

Henley Royal Regatta

SMALL *Oxford* BOOKS

BOATING

Compiled by
CHRISTOPHER DODD

Oxford   New York
OXFORD UNIVERSITY PRESS
1983

Oxford University Press, Walton Street, Oxford OX2 6DP

London Glasgow New York Toronto
Delhi Bombay Calcutta Madras Karachi
Kuala Lumpur Singapore Hong Kong Tokyo
Nairobi Dar es Salaam Cape Town
Melbourne Auckland

and associate companies in
Beirut Berlin Ibadan Mexico City

British Library Cataloguing in Publication Data

Boating.—(Small Oxford books)
1. Rowing—Anecdotes, facetiae, satire, etc.
I. Dodd, Christopher
797.1'23   GV791
ISBN 0-19-214138-4

Library of Congress Cataloging in Publication Data

Main entry under title:
Boating
(Small Oxford Books)
Includes index
1. Boats and boating—Anecdotes, facetiae, satire, etc.
I. Dodd, Christopher
GV777.3.B6 1983   797.1   82-12531
ISBN 0-19-214138-4 (U.S.)

Set by New Western Printing Ltd
Printed in Great Britain by
Hazell Watson & Viney Limited
Aylesbury, Bucks

To Ratty and Mole
and all who scull with them

Introduction

To the lucky among us, boating means messing about in a skiff. Or to the unlucky, skiffing around in a mess. To most people, however, rowing means the Boat Race and eccentric goings on at Henley. The first hogs the publicity and the second is the showcase, at least as far as Britain is concerned. The two events are colourful manifestations of a sport which was developed before most others and which has its roots in other ages and other continents. The English can claim the seed-sowing of both amateur and professional rowing and sculling for sport and pleasure, and for popularizing and spreading their recreation wherever they ventured as explorers, entrepreneurs, or imperialists. For some peoples the oar has been as significant as the wheel for the development of mobility and commerce. The powerful nations of antiquity rowed and moved very large vessels by the oar, the lever which moves a boat through water. He who had only a paddle was at a disadvantage, applying motive power indirectly through his body. The rower applies power through the rowlock or a similar device directly to the boat. Thus a history of rowing would have to start among the Egyptians and take in the Assyrians, Phoenicians, Greeks, and Romans, with their cargo fleets and their military galleys, before examining the river lore and transport of Europe and the complementary role of the oar to sail and wind power.

This little book does not attempt such a grandiose plan. Much has been left out, hence its necessary in-completeness, its indiscipline fit to make a captain wince. From the time when the use of oars among watermen began to decline as bridges and steam and internal combustion turned the men into tugmen and cabbies, from the time when the boys of Eton and Westminster spread their daredevil waterborne fun to the ancient universities, and the Tynesiders raced for stakes and turned their talents to boat and accessory design, there has been a dedicated platoon of scribes putting down the who, what, where, when, and why of rowing, and many of them have been as clear, literate, and funny as others have been fuddled, muddled, and dour.

Neither they nor their subject-matter can get into a small space, so admittance to these pages has been pretty random. There is a taste of the galley and the Thames, a song of the Tyne, a hint of the training and toughness, the comradeship and philistinism, the culture and religious fervour variously claimed or denied. There is a meandering journey on far-flung waters, a dip-and-bucket through fact and fiction, time and pace. The collection is as rambling as an up-river regatta, but the organizer hopes for sunshine, fresh air, fellowship, and a couple of good races.

This is not, by and large, an occasion for champions, records, definitions, coaching manuals, or debates of style. It is, you might say, a sideways glance at the art of facing backwards in order to move forwards. It's a celebration of a beautiful and healthy sport which grew out of more serious motives, and it's a bow in recognition of some of Britain's oldest sporting institutions. The Amateur Rowing Association, founded in 1882 and the governing body for England and Wales, is young compared with Henley (1839) or the Boat Race (1829) or Thomas Doggett's Coat and Badge (1716). As long as they all keep pulling, the ARA will, happily, never catch up.

───── ❧ ─────

Messing About

───── ❧ ─────

'Nice? It's the *only* thing,' said the Water Rat solemnly, as he leant forward for his stroke. 'Believe me, my young friend, there is *nothing* – absolutely nothing – half so much worth doing as simply messing about in boats. Simply messing,' he went on dreamily: 'messing – about – in – boats; messing – '

'Look ahead, Rat!' cried the Mole suddenly.

It was too late. The boat struck the bank full tilt. The dreamer, the joyous oarsman, lay on his back at the bottom of the boat, his heels in the air.

' – about in boats – or *with* boats,' the Rat went on composedly, picking himself up with a pleasant laugh. 'In or out of 'em, it doesn't matter. Nothing seems really to matter, that's the charm of it. Whether you get away, or whether you don't; whether you arrive at your destination or whether you reach somewhere else, or whether you never get anywhere at all, you're always busy, and you never do anything in particular; and when you've done it there's always something else to do, and you can do it if you like, but you'd much better not. Look here! If you've really nothing else on hand this morning, supposing we drop down the river together, and have a long day of it?'

Kenneth Grahame, *The Wind in the Willows*, 1908

Racing and getting about is only a part of rowing and sculling. Boating can mean holidays and picnic days, best personified in fiction by Jerome K. Jerome in Three Men in a Boat, *and in fact by Dr Frederick Furnivall who used to take Sunday trips between Hammersmith and Kingston, come hell or high water.*

The Victorians in particular took to boating like ducks to water, witness the Oxford boat-builders John and Stephen Salter's advertisement in 1871 :

A large selection, both new and second-hand, kept in readiness for Sale or Hire, consisting of Eight, Four, Pair-oar and Sculling Outriggers, Gigs, Whiffs, Canoes, *large and small Pleasure Boats, Skiffs, Punts, and Dinghies, suitable for Lakes and Ornamental Waters,* Centre-board Sailing Boats, Oars, Sculls, Sails, Cushions, Boat-varnish &c.

An hour in a punt or a week on the Thames jammed in colourful crushes in the locks or lining the course at a regatta was all good grist to the Victorians. Jerome's three men were kitted out and victualled fit for a houseboat or a steam launch for their trip, which began in a manner closely resembling the preparations for a rowing tour of the Danube, Moldau, and Elbe described here :

The crew consisted of the skipper, my brother, hereafter called 'Stroke', and myself. The skipper had earned his title by varied experiences of British and foreign water-ways. Stroke had nearly the same record. I had rowed in my Oxford College boat, but the continent was *terra incognita*, so I gladly agreed to join them on a cruise down the Danube, the Moldau, and the Elbe. Danube scenery is well-known to English travellers and readers, but the Moldau has not been so often explored or so eloquently praised, though its splendid reaches and intricate navigation afford equal pleasure to the oars-man. Preliminaries were arranged at my brother's club, and a fortnight later we met again at the skipper's house on the evening previous to our start. Here the details of the route were discussed, and the baggage packed, namely: first, one waterproof 'Cording' bag each, containing the minimum articles for daily use. These bags serve also as life-buoys in case of need. Secondly, a 'tosh' bag with all the waterproofs and tools for repairing damage. Thirdly, a handy, joint swagger bag, with the shore-going clothes, as it is a refreshment to change everything after a day's work, and we prefer appearing at the *table d'hôte* and in the towns as not being of a boat, boaty. Lastly, the 'Captain's bag', a small one, with maps, guide-books, pipes, flasks, cork-screw, and any small articles used on a voyage, and likely to be wanted at a moment's notice.

Thursday, 13th August, was the day of final preparation. We dined at my brother's chambers, called a growler, and were off.

Revd A. F. Ryder Bird, *Boating in Austria, Bavaria, and Bohemia*, 1893

Once the party is assembled and under way, some mug must be found to do the work:

You can always tell the old river hand by the way in which he stretches himself out upon the cushions at the bottom of the boat, and encourages the rowers by telling them anecdotes about the marvellous feats he performed last season.

'Call what you're doing hard work?' he drawls, between his contented whiffs, addressing the two perspiring novices, who have been grinding away steadily up-stream for the last hour and a half; 'why, Jim Biffles and Jack and I, last season, pulled up from Marlow to Goring in one afternoon – never stopped once. Do you remember that, Jack?'

Jack, who has made himself a bed, in the prow, of all the rugs and coats he can collect, and who has been lying there asleep for the last two hours, partially wakes up on being thus appealed to, and recollects all about the matter, and also remembers that there was an un-usually strong stream against them all the way – likewise a stiff wind.

'About thirty-four miles, I suppose, it must have been,' adds the first speaker, reaching down another cushion to put under his head.

'No – no; don't exaggerate, Tom,' murmurs Jack, reprovingly; 'thirty-three at the outside.'

And Jack and Tom, quite exhausted by this conversational effort, drop off to sleep once more. And the two simple-minded youngsters at the skulls feel quite proud of being allowed to row such wonderful oarsmen as Jack and Tom, and strain away harder than ever.

Jerome K. Jerome, *Three Men in a Boat*, 1889

Dr Furnivall was a scholar and in his young days a builder of experimental sculling boats with outriggers, a development not wholly attributable to him but one which enabled rowing to be done with effect in lightweight and very narrow boats. He founded Furnivall Sculling Club in Hammersmith and inveigled everyone he met from his professorial colleagues to the waitresses at his favourite ABC café to learn to scull and join his picnic parties. He

*became the most familiar figure on the top end of the
Tideway before his death in 1910; Jessie Currie's experience of him was typical:*

When I took a studio at No. 4 St George's Square,
Primrose Hill, the outgoing tenant said, 'Let me intro-
duce you to Dr Furnivall. He will ask you if you can
scull. If you say "No", he will take you up the river to
teach you. If you say "Yes", he will take you up the
river to keep you in practice. He will take you, anyhow.'

I well remember my first impression of the Doctor –
his keen eye, large brow, and militant moustache. He
seemed to look me through almost at a glance, and to
give me my particular place amongst his acquaintances.

I could not help smiling as, after a little inquiry
about my work, he asked, 'Can you scull?' When I
answered 'Yes', his whole face beamed. 'How jolly!' he
exclaimed. 'I hope you will often come up the river
with us.' . . .

Few people would have known that some of the
greatest living scholars were often in the Doctor's boat,
as we sculled up from Richmond to Canbury Island,
near Kingston-on-Thames. Here we would have lunch
under the trees; and after lunch came 'washing up', at
which we all assisted, the Doctor superintending the
while. This done, the Doctor generally rested for about
an hour on the grass, whilst the younger members of
the party sculled the boat on either side of the island –
sometimes sending a friendly call to him as he lay near
the water's edge, to which he would respond by shaking
his foot in the air.

Later on, he would beckon to the boat, which pulled
in and took him across to the cottage, where we took
in great teapots full of tea, and jugs of milk, and brought
them over to the island. Some of the party meanwhile
had spread the cloth, cut bread and butter, opened

pots of jam, and divided the cakes. The 'club' girls from Hammersmith arrived about tea-time and the island was gay with fluttering dresses, white flannels, table-cloths, and bright boat-cushions, whilst the air was full of chatter and laughter and the pleasant sound of tea-things.

Jessie Currie, *Memories of F. J. Furnivall*, 1921

Charles Dodgson, alias Lewis Carroll, found inspiration on boating trips with little Alice Liddell and her sisters:

At Folly Bridge Dodgson chose a boat with his usual meticulousness. This time they could not go to Nuneham, for picnickers were not allowed to land there on a Friday. Instead, they rowed up the river in the opposite direction to Godstowe, a journey whick took them all of two and a half hours.

As usual the three children were stowed away in the stern. 'I rowed *stroke* and he rowed *bow* . . . and the story was actually composed *over my shoulder* for the benefit of Alice Liddell, who was acting as "cox" of our gig,' wrote Robinson Duckworth, many years later. 'I remember turning round and saying, "Dodgson, is this an extempore romance of yours?" And he replied, "Yes, I'm inventing as we go along."'

Alice, too, retained clear recollections of that historic outing:

The beginning of *Alice* was told to me one summer afternoon when the sun was so hot we landed in meadows down the river, deserting the boat to take refuge in the only bit of shade to be found, which was under a newly made hayrick. Here from all three of us, my sisters and myself, came the old petition, 'Tell us a story,' and Mr Dodgson (that is Lewis Carroll) began it.

Sometimes to tease us, Mr Dodgson would stop and say suddenly, 'That's all till next time.' 'Oh,' we would cry, 'It's not bedtime already' and he would go on.

[6]

Another time the story would begin in the boat and Mr Dodgson would pretend to fall asleep in the middle, to our great dismay.

A quarter of a century later Dodgson himself also recalled the occasion:

Many a day we rowed together on that quiet stream – the three little maidens and I – and many a fairy tale had been extemporised for their benefit – whether it were at times when the narrator was 'i' the vein', and fancies unsought came crowding thick upon him, or at times when the jaded Muse was goaded into action, and plodded meekly on, more because she had to say something than because she had something to say – yet none of these many tales got written down: they lived and died, like summer midges, each in its own golden afternoon until there came a day when, as it chanced, one of my little listeners petitioned that the tale might be written out for her.

Anne Clark, *The Real Alice*, 1981

> All in the golden afternoon
> Full leisurely we glide;
> For both our oars, with little skill,
> By little arms are plied,
> While little hands make vain pretence
> Our wanderings to guide.

Lewis Carroll, *Alice's Adventures in Wonderland*, 1865

Boating is not all fun. It can be a hazardous business when you don't know what you're doing, or when the other chap doesn't know what you or he is doing, or according to Mr Jerome when girls are involved, or when steam launches or their modern equivalents are about. Here is Martin Cobbett, a famous sports journalist of late-Victorian and Edwardian days, on the confusion that the righteous can get into when someone doesn't hug the bank going against the stream, or keep to the middle going with it :

[7]

I only wish I could be strong-minded enough to stand on my rights, even if that meant getting my boat smashed up and my precious person cast into the water. Very unpleasant that is – I have 'tried 'em both' – yet, all the same, there is your duty straight afore you, and you ought to go for it to the extent of declining to steer out of your proper course to suit the convenience of others who are very much off theirs. Sometimes I get so vexed and humiliated, that I could punch my own head for being the ass I am to allow people to humbug me about. For there is fate in it. Who gets put in he wrong and feels the position keenly? I do.

Does the offending party mind who, coming up zigzag-wise in the middle of the river, meets me going down where I ought to be, and after various misleading manoeuvres causes me to steer in towards the bank as the only way of avoiding collision? Does he, do his pals, care a tinker's curse about what I say? Not a ha'porth. Likely enough he believes himself quite a martyr, being talked to after all his politeness.

And what happens to me? Scooting out of the intruder's way I am forced near to the bank, and of course get into a mix with incredulous gentlemen working up in the orthodox manner. 'The middle of the stream going down, sir,' says someone with vitriolic politeness. 'How they get trusted with a boat at all I can't understand,' puts in another. 'Did you think you were going up or down the river?' is a question not meant altogether kindly.

Explanation is vain, and you are obliged to take and swallow insult which really you do deserve for not doing the right thing at the outset by refusing to budge from your right course.

Martin Cobbett, Sporting Notions, 1908

There are ways of taming monsters ...

There is a blatant bumptiousness about a steam-launch, that has the knack of rousing every evil instinct in my nature, and I yearn for the good old days, when you could go about and tell people what you thought of them with a hatchet and a bow and arrows. The expression on the face of the man who, with his hands in his pockets, stands by the stern, smoking a cigar, is sufficient to excuse a breach of the peace by itself; and the lordly whistle for you to get out of the way would, I am confident, ensure a verdict of 'justifiable homicide' from any jury of river-men.

They used to *have* to whistle for us to get out of their way. If I may do so, without appearing boastful, I think I can honestly say that our one small boat, during that week, caused more annoyance and delay and aggravation to the steam-launches that we came across than all the other craft on the river put together.

'Steam-launch coming!' one of us would cry out, on sighting the enemy in the distance; and in an instant, everything was got ready to receive her. I would take the lines, and Harris and George would sit down beside me, all of us with our backs to the launch, and the boat would drift out quietly into midstream.

On would come the launch, whistling, and on we would go, drifting. At about a hundred yards off, she would start whistling like mad, and the people would come and lean over the side, and roar at us; but we never heard them! Harris would be telling us an anecdote about his mother, and George and I would not have missed a word of it for worlds.

Then that launch would give one final shriek of a whistle that would nearly burst the boiler, and she would reverse her engines, and blow off steam, and swing round and get aground; everyone on board of it would rush to the bow and yell at us, and the people on the bank would stand and shout at us, and all the other passing boats would stop and join in, till the whole river for miles up and down was in a state of frantic commotion. And then Harris would break off in the most interesting part of his narrative and look up with mild surprise, and say to George:

'Why, George, bless us, if here isn't a steam-launch!'

And George would answer:

'Well, do you know, I *thought* I heard something!'

Upon which we would get nervous and confused, and not know how to get the boat out of the way, and the people in the launch would crowd round and instruct us:

'Pull your right – you, you idiot! Back with your left. No, not *you* – the other one – leave the lines alone, can't you – now, both together. NOT *that* way. Oh, you – !'

Then they would lower a boat and come to our assistance; and, after a quarter of an hour's effort, would get us clean out of their way, so that they could go on; and we would thank them so much, and ask them to give us a tow. But they never would.

Another good way we discovered of irritating the aristocratic type of steam-launch, was to mistake them for a beanfeast, and ask them if they were Messrs Cubitt's lot or the Bermondsey Good Templars, and could they lend us a saucepan.

Jerome K. Jerome, *Three Men in a Boat*, 1889

. . . and of making use of them :

At Reading lock we came up with a steam-launch, belonging to some friends of mine, and they towed us up to within about a mile of Streatley. It is very delightful being towed up by a launch. I prefer it myself to rowing. The run would have been more delightful still, if it had not been for a lot of wretched small boats that were continually getting in the way of our launch, and, to avoid running down which, we had to be continually easing and stopping. It is really most annoying, the manner in which these rowing boats get in the way of one's launch up the river; something ought to be done to stop it.

And they are so confoundedly impertinent, too, over it. You can whistle till you nearly burst your boiler before they will trouble themselves to hurry. I would have one or two of them run down now and then, if I had my way, just to teach them all a lesson.

Jerome K. Jerome, *Three Men in a Boat*, 1889

Boating people naturally assume that rivers and lakes are theirs by right. Those with rods, skis, motors, and even sails can keep clear or better still, keep off. Hazards are not always from humans, however. Foolish is he who has no respect for the swan:

Being quite lonely, I had a turn spying up and down the reach above the long eyot of old Windsor in search of my friend the enemy, a nasty, disagreeable, cantankerous, aged master-swan, and wasted twenty minutes before I recollected that he was happily killed ten years ago. He *was* a brute, but in the matter of company, a live beast without extenuating circumstances is better to have a row with than no one to contradict you. I should not have taken so kindly interest in the gentleman had I been in a boat. He used to come at you if he travelled a quarter of a mile to do it. Once the villain surpassed himself. I hope I never shall get into such a pickle again. His mastership took to flying, and there was I sculling for dear life with this chap 'whanging' along, his evil head and great long neck stretched at me over the stern of the boat.

Martin Cobbett, *Sporting Notions*, 1908

Pursued by swans or cut up on the water by cantankerous young men, Cobbett missed very little that moved on the Thames. He once reported that the brothers Louch ran a steam-launch called the Black Watch *up over Marlow weir against the stream during flood time. The men who went adventuring on the Danube shot weirs in their rowing boat, a riskier business :*

No weirs to-day so far, but just as we are congratulating ourselves thereon, we see a mill, barrage, and weir. It has a 'long drop', but is open; we inspect it, lighten the boat, and Stroke volunteers to shoot it alone, not without some anxiety on the part of all as to the result. As before, there is first the drop on to the shoot or apron, and then the descent from the apron to the waves and rushing water. Stroke judged his distance accurately; Skipper and I watch, one on each side; the boat comes bounding over like a deer, seems to hesitate a little as her keel touched the apron, and then leapt on into the curling wave, and after struggling with it for a moment, came up and out in triumph.

Revd A. F. Ryder Bird, Boating in Austria, Bavaria,
and Bohemia, 1893

Weirs, often called lashers on the Thames, are hazardous at the best of times; punting runs the risk of stranding the punter on top of his pole while his punt cruises off minus means of propulsion. Moving a houseboat combines all the risks as Theodore Cook and his friends found out when they hired the little Midge *from Salters at Folly Bridge, Oxford, and took her downstream to a mooring just below Fawley on the famous Henley Regatta course:*

Economy was perforce our motto, so we started down from Folly Bridge (that is its real name) one summer afternoon not long after our third Commemoration, and using no other means of guidance and propulsion than a tow-rope and punt-pole, set forth for Iffley, and in due time arrived at Sandford, where we dined and drank old ale – a brew which made us wonder why so much fuss was ever made about the Trinity Audit of our light-blue rivals.

That must have been about 1888. We unslung the Canadian canoe from our upper decks, stepped a bamboo mast, hoisted a red triangle of silken sail, and scudded before a light breeze in the moonlight down the Radley reaches. When and how we got back to the *Midge* to bed I mind not. But while we slept a summer storm must have arisen. The *Midge*, taking command herself, must have slipped softly and slowly downstream, guided by some friendly Nereid; for we awoke, as the dawn flushed the Nuneham trees with gold, with a terrific bump as her stern swung heavily into the railway bridge a mile or so above Abingdon Lasher. We rose with joyful unconcern, and towed and punted her in our pyjamas until that ancient town came into sight and then tied up (a trifle tighter than before) for breakfast.

I remember there was some cheering when (five days later!) we got perilously and safely through Henley Bridge, and amid applause, which a decadent Press might have described as ironical, we moved slowly down the gorgeous line of houseboats and slipped at last into our own position. Supper that night was a mixed contribution from our charitable neighbours, for nothing to eat or drink was left on board, and we were far too lazy, after our last long traverse, to go back to the town and fetch any. The language of the man who began to drink our last teaspoonful of kerosene, under the impression there was whisky in his water, stays in my memory yet.

One of our crew is now Sir Robert Giles, Vice-Chancellor of the University of Burmah and Speaker of the Council of Representatives in Rangoon. He had already developed the habits proper to a magnate in the tropics, and refused to let anyone except Urwick be entrusted with washing up the plates.

T. A. Cook, *The Sunlit Hours*, 1925

The Professionals

Quinquireme of Nineveh from distant Ophir
Rowing home to haven in sunny Palestine,
With a cargo of ivory,
And apes and peacocks,
Sandalwood, cedarwood, and sweet white wine.

John Masefield, from 'Cargoes', 1902

*Greeks, Romans, and other Mediterranean peoples de-
ployed fleets of galleys equipped with up to three banks of
oars. Most were for military use, some designed primarily
as rammers and others as grapplers and troop-ships. The
most advanced designs were catamarans carrying large
catapults. The galleys are classified according to the
number of oarsmen manning a bank of oars in echelon on
one side of the boat. For example, a trireme has three oars
with one man on each, whereas the quinquireme referred
to in Masefield's poem probably has one man on the lowest
oar and two men on the middle and upper oars respectively.
Ptolemy IV built a twin-hulled tessarakonteres, or forty,
near the end of the 3rd century BC, manned by 4,000
oarsmen and carrying 2,850 troops and 400 deckhands.
Here, however, is an attempt to compare the performance
of a common trireme with a modern racing eight over the
Boat Race course of four and a quarter miles:*

Comparisons between a trireme's speed and that of a
rowing eight can be only approximate because much
depends on the distance. A good crew in the University
Boat Race, where there is varying tide assistance, is
thought to be making about 10 knots through the water.

A fraction over 11 knots has been done at Henley. According to the Guinness Book of Records, the world record for an eight over 2,000 metres is the 13.46 mph (about $11\frac{1}{4}$ knots) achieved by the East Germans at Montreal in 1976.

So, in a Putney to Mortlake race on a calm day, an educated guess might well conjecture a quarter-mile victory by the trireme over Oxford and Cambridge. As for really choppy Thames weather, however, the evidence from Xenophon and others is that Greek oarsmen shrewdly avoided such conditions. They would stay in the clubhouse.

Roy Perrott, *The Sunday Times*, 26 April 1981

One of the most famous long-distance trireme dashes took place in 427 BC :

The city of Mitylene on the island of Lesbos had revolted against its Athenian masters and had then been retaken. The Athenian demagogue Cleon proposed that the entire population of the subject city be put to death, and his rhetoric carried the day in the public assembly. Accordingly a trireme was sent out to carry the order to the Athenian garrison. Given the high state of political passions in Athens, it probably set out early in the afternoon, soon after the assembly vote. As Thucydides writes, however, because of the horrid nature of its errand, it made no haste. Cruising on one or two banks and setting a slow stroke, it probably made no more than four or five knots.

The next morning the assembly met again, cooler heads prevailed and the massacre order was repealed. Hoping for this change, the Mitylenian ambassadors in Athens had arranged for a fast ship and a crack crew, providing them with high-energy foods for the trip and promising large sums of money if they could catch the first galley before its dispatch could be carried out.

The second ship apparently left for Lesbos, a trip of some 345 kilometres, about 24 hours after the first. It made the open sea before nightfall, and the crew rowed continuously through the night. They were even fed as they rowed, with wine-moistened barley cakes. The night was clear enough for navigation and there was no head wind. In order to maximize their speed the commanders either took on enough rowers for an extra bank to rotate with the original three or kept two full banks out of three going continuously in watches during the night, with the third sleeping. Whichever technique was used, they reached Mitylene at midday, just after the arrival of the first galley. It appears, therefore, that they spent less than 24 hours in transit, cruising at close to nine knots (16.6 kilometres per hour). The dispatch had been delivered but the garrison had not had time to begin putting it into effect. A modern ferry makes the trip in 14 hours.

Vernard Foley and Werner Soedel, Scientific American,
1981

During his adventures in the Aeneid, *Aeneas organizes a galley race which exhibits much of the glory and some of the gory of the galley business. It is between four captains – Gyas, Cloanthus, Mnestheus, and Sergestus, and as we join it Gyas has already been passed:*

And now hope was joyously reawakened in the last two competitors, Sergestus and Mnestheus, who, since Gyas had encountered this delay, saw a chance of passing him. Sergestus took the open sea-room first, in front of Mnestheus, and drew near the rock. However, he was leading not by a whole keel's length but by a part only, for the Pristis [Mnestheus' galley] pressed him, moving alongside in keen competition. Meanwhile Mnestheus walked down his ship among the crew, encouraging them: 'Rise to the oars! In! Out! You who

were once the comrades of Hector! You whom I chose
to be mine at Troy's last fated hour! Show us now the
strength and spirit which you showed in past perils . . .'

A mere accident brought the brave crew the honour
for which they longed. For Sergestus, wild with excitement, forced his bow close up to the rocks on the
inside of Mnestheus, and forging on with insufficient
sea-room by ill luck ran aground on a jutting reef. The
rock-crag shuddered. Oars, strained against the sharp
edges, snapped noisily; the prow, driven ashore, hung
poised. At this check the crew leapt up and shouted
loudly. Then they unshipped iron-headed poles and
sharp-pointed boat-hooks and rescued broken oars in
the water. But Mnestheus was now exultant and all the
more energetic for the improvement in his position. He
made for the home waters ahead, with his oars pulling
in rapid rhythm, and also with winds now behind him
in answer to his prayer; and so he swiftly sped across
open sea towards land. Next he drew level with Gyas
and his vast, massive Chimaera, which being deprived
of her helmsman now lost her lead.

So only Cloanthus, alone and nearing the finish, was
left. Mnestheus tore after him, pressing him, and
straining with every ounce of strength. Now, of course,
the shouting redoubled. The watchers all in high excitement urged on the pursuer and the sky rang with their
outbursts. The one crew were bitterly fearing that they
might not, after all, retain a glory which they had
counted their own as surely as if their honour was
already won, and would willingly have accepted fame
at the cost of life itself. The other crew were
strengthened by the taste of success, and confidence
gave them power. Indeed, both crews might perhaps
have shared the prize with prows finishing level, if
Cloanthus had not uttered a passionate prayer, and,
stretching both palms towards the ocean, called on the

gods to accept his vows: 'Gods who are sovereign over the ocean, Gods on whose sea-surface I sail, if you answer my prayer I shall joyfully station at an altar on this coast a bull of glistening white for you, and I shall cast the entrails as offerings to the salt waves and pour out streams of clear wine.' Thus he prayed. And deep below the waves all the dancing band of Phorcus, all the Nereids, and maiden Panopea, heard; and old Father Portunus himself thrust onwards the moving ship with his own large hands. And so she sped to the land, swifter than the south wind, swifter than a flying arrow, and passed from sight within the spacious harbour.

So Anchises' son following the custom called all together. His herald's loud voice declared Cloanthus the victor, and Aeneas set a wreath of green bay-leaves on his brow. He then presented prizes to be distributed among the crews according to their own choice, three bullocks for each ship, wine, and the fine possession of a large-size silver talent.

They had all received their presentations and were moving off with scarlet ribbons on their brows in exultation at their rich prizes, when, having barely, and with much ingenuity, extricated himself from the cruel rock, Sergestus, with some of his oars gone and one whole tier out of action, brought his ship in with no acclaim but only mockery. She was like a snake, caught as they often are on the bank beside a road, either run over by a bronze wheel, or torn with a stone angrily flung by some traveller and left mangled and only half-alive; trying in vain to escape, it twists in long spasms, for in a part of itself it has life yet, and, though the rest of it, maimed by the wound, drags helplessly, and it can only writhe in knots and fold back on itself, its eyes still blaze and the hissing neck is still held high. Such was the state of the ship's oarage, and it slowed her movement; but she spread her canvas in spite of all and under full sail moved up to the harbour-mouth. And Aeneas, glad that Sergestus had saved his ship and brought his crew home, presented him with the prize which he had offered. He gave him a Cretan slave-girl, named Pholoe, clever at Minerva's tasks and nursing twin baby boys.

Virgil (70–19 BC), *The Aeneid*

Rowing in echelon had unexpected problems identified by Aristophanes :

The close packing of the rowers in the hull was further effected by arranging them in echelon, with the top men sitting about half a metre ahead of those in the middle bank and the middle men in turn about the same distance above and ahead of the men in the hold. The men were closely packed in each layer too, with only about a metre's space between them. This meant that if someone was rowing even slightly out of time, he would drive his back into the knuckles of the man at his rear or his knuckles into the back of the man in front.

The men rowing in the hold had a further clearance problem. As the comic playwright Aristophanes remarked in his play *The Frogs*, their noses came close to the bottoms of the men seated just above and ahead of

them as they reached forward to begin their stroke.
The effort of the pull sometimes made the rowers break
wind at just this moment.

Vernard Foley and Werner Soedel, *Scientific American*,
1981

Not much has been written about rowing by either Vikings
or oarsmen from the ancient world, partly because of their
illiteracy and partly because rowing was such a fundamen-
tal way of moving or at least steering a ship that its tech-
nicalities may have been regarded as commonplace.
Contrary to popular belief, the Greeks and Romans used
slaves to row their ships only in extremis. *Oarsmen needed*
to be in prime condition. They were often privileged free-
men, kept on a good diet and high pay. Their lifestyle
may well have approached that of the international com-
petitor of the 1980s, well looked after by coaches, diet-
itians, doctors, and physiotherapists, sponsored and
managed. All, that is, except for the French, who kept
squadrons of galleys in the Med and the Channel into the
eighteenth century. They manned them with convicts,
Turkish mercenaries, and persecuted Huguenots. One of
the latter recorded his appalling life in Galley Slave.
Here Jean Marteilhe describes life under the officers and
comité, *the chief petty officer, the officers' lapdog and the*
curse of the crew :

The *comités* pass on every order [by the boatswain's
pipe] after having received the captain's instructions.
Each manoeuvre, and each particular task, is directed
by a different call. Even individuals, indicated by their
duties, are addressed by them; and those who hear these
calls without understanding them think they hear
nightingales singing. I remember that our *comité* once
had a skylark in a cage. This creature learned to sing
the different calls so well that it sometimes made us do
things which had never been ordered, and the captain

had to tell the *comité* to get rid of the bird, for it allowed us no rest.

Jean Marteilhe, Galley Slave, 18th century

In The Finest Story in the World *Rudyard Kipling describes the friendship between a writer who realizes that a young clerk with whom he strikes a friendship is the re-incarnation of what he supposes to be a galley slave with experience of both Vikings and Mediterranean ships. He wrestles some of the details of young Charlie's other lives :*

We pulled for you when the wind was against us and the sails were low.

Will you never let us go?

We ate bread and onions when you took towns, or ran aboard quickly when you were beaten back by the foe,

The captains walked up and down the deck in fair weather singing songs, but we were below.

We fainted with our chins on the oars and you did not see that we were idle, for we still swung to and fro.

Will you never let us go?

The salt made the oar-handles like shark-skin; our knees were cut to the bone with salt-cracks; our hair was stuck to our foreheads; and our lips were cut to our gums, and you whipped us because we could not row.

Will you never let us go?

But in a little time we shall run out of the portholes as the water runs along the oar-blade, and though you tell the others to row after us you will never catch us till you catch the oar-thresh and tie up the winds in the belly of the sail. Aho!

Will you never let us go?

'H'm. What's oar-thresh, Charlie?'

'The water washed up by the oars. That's the sort of song they might sing in the galley y'know.'

Rudyard Kipling, The Finest Story in the World, 1891

Galleys were useless in rough weather, priceless against becalmed sailing ships. The French hunted in packs attacking Dutch and English convoys in the Channel, and they were highly disciplined and manœuvrable. They were capable of sporting attempts at planing as well, although not with the active enjoyment of the horny-handed sons of toil:

On one occasion our galley was at Boulogne, near Calais, where the duc d'Aumont, whom we later saw as ambassador to the court of England, was living at that time. Monsieur de Langeron entertained him on board, and as the sea was very smooth and he wished to give pleasure to this gentleman, he suggested a cruise, which was accepted.

We rowed easily almost to Dover and the duke, thinking of the heavy work and the miserable condition of the slaves, remarked that he could not understand how such wretches were able to sleep, being so tightly packed and with nothing to lie down upon. 'I know well enough,' answered the captain, 'how to make them sleep soundly, and this evening I shall convince you of it by a good dose of opium which I shall prepare for them!' He then called the *comité* and gave him orders to put about and return to Boulogne. Wind and tide were against us and we were ten leagues from this port. When we had turned, the captain ordered full speed and *passe-vogue*. This is the most awful thing it is possible to imagine – it doubles the speed of the rowing stroke, and one hour of it is more exhausting than four of ordinary rowing. Besides, in the *passe-vogue* it is impossible to avoid often missing a stroke, and then the lashes fall like hail.

We finally arrived at Boulogne, but so exhausted and distressed by blows that we could scarcely move arms or legs. The captain then ordered the *comité* to make the slaves lie down, which was done by a call of the pipe. The duc d'Aumont and the officers dined, and when they rose from the table after midnight the captain said to the duke that he wished to show him the effect of his opium and led him along the *coursier*, from whence they could see the poor slaves, the greater number of whom were asleep; but others were unable to close an eye on account of their sufferings, although they pretended to sleep, for so the captain had ordered, not wishing that his opium should seem without the effect he had promised the duke. But what a horrible spectacle he offered his guest! Six wretches on every bench crouched up and piled one upon another, all naked, for not one had the strength to put on his shirt. Most of them were all blood from the lashes they had received, and they were covered with perspiration. 'You see, monsieur,' said the captain, 'have I not the secret of how to make these fellows sleep? And I shall also show you that I know how to awaken them.' He then ordered the *comités* to pipe the reveille, and then there was seen the saddest sight in the world – hardly one of the slaves could raise himself up, so stiff were their legs and bodies: and they were only made to do so by great lashes, twisting themselves into a thousand ridiculous and agonized postures. From such an example one may judge the captains and senior officers to be as cruel as the *comités* themselves.

Jean Marteilhe, *Galley Slave*, 18th century

Thames Tideway

Let your oars like lightning flog it,
Up the Thames as swiftly jog it,
And you'd win the prize of Doggett,
The Glory of the river.
Bendin! bowing; strainin; rowin;
Perhaps the wind in fury blowin;
Or the tide again you flowin;
The Coat and Badge for ever.

Anonymous waterman

Doggett's Coat and Badge was started by the Irish actor Thomas Doggett in 1715, supposedly to commemorate the Hanoverian accession. It is a sculling race from London Bridge to Chelsea, originally for watermen in their first year of freedom from apprenticeship, and is still run today thanks to the provision of Doggett's will. The winner still receives a scarlet coat, hat, and knee-breeches, and a large silver badge worn on the arm. At one time the Thames employed tens of thousands of watermen running a cab service in pair-oars or single-manned boats, and the livery companies and wealthy aristocrats had their own ceremonial barges. The Lord Mayor's Show was originally a water pageant. The very life of London as a port was bound up with watermen and rowing and out of it grew a thriving professional side to the sport in the nineteenth century which, competitively speaking, died out by the Second World War. Here is James Bone on Britain's oldest continuous competitive sporting event (which now has amateur status):

Our complement on the good steamer *Pepys* was partly made up by coalmen from Erith, bargees from Limehouse, rogue riderhoods, and other riverside characters. Five aquatic bookmakers were in attendance, and on the inviolate Thames fearlessly shouted the odds in the beard of the pier policeman. Pocock of Eton, Joe Beckett of 'Lime'us,' Young Jeffries of Erith, and Rough of Putney were the fancied ones, and Gibson and Bland were any odds you liked. Pocock, however, was the big favourite, and he showed himself the winner from the first, his big long body in dark green getting clean away at the start (the rest were 'the fie-uld', by the way, not the 'water' or 'the river', as the aquatic bookmakers should have known). It would take the Water Poet himself to sing the glories of that great race. Everyone agreed that no man could wish to see a better race till the day he died. Off went Pocock in the centre of the river, tossing the spray as high as his head before he steadied to it. Beckett, in white, was close behind, and Rough next. Pocock shot Southwark Bridge well ahead, with the river fairly clear before him, the steamers hurrying well behind, and dodging round a couple of dumb barges with sweeps out, he went through Blackfriars easily. In the long stretch to Waterloo the race came on a fleet of seven sail of compressed hay well in the fairway, and just at Waterloo we saw that Rough had slipped inside of them, and in smoother water was shooting the southmost arch of the bridge at the same time as Pocock. And so the race went on through the river traffic, each man guiding himself as best he could. At Charing Cross one year the leader found himself suddenly hoist on a whirlpool, made by the escaped air from the tunnelling deep below for the Bakerloo tube, but there was no such accident this time. Nor was any competitor struck on the head by a bottle nor pulled out of his boat with boat-hooks by the well-wishers of another competitor, nor upset by them. These things have happened in the Doggett, but it's a long time ago. Nor was any man even impeded on his lawful occasion. High on the bridge of the *Queen Elizabeth*, which carried a worshipful Company of Fishmongers, stood a man in a cocked hat with a port-wine coat and light blue trousers and a gold badge like a tray on his arm. He was the bargemaster of the company and the father of Pocock, yet never once did he run down any of his son's rivals, nor give them his wash more than is customary. Pocock won by half a dozen lengths, covering the four and a half miles in thirty-three minutes, and he took a turn up the river before he lifted his 6 feet 3 inches of young manhood into the launch. Jeffries and Gibson, who had kept within three lengths of one another for half the course, making spurt after spurt and reducing even the coalmen to speechlessness, so that they couldn't in the end say, '*Dig it boy – dig it – dig it, my bully boy – hoorah*,' had to be taken from their boats. The giant young waterman had rowed them out.

James Bone, *The London Perambulator*, 1925

The boys of Westminster School were pioneers of amateur rowing, boating from the Horseferry before the Embankment was built and having occasional matches with Eton. They were up to mischief on the Thames in the early part of last century:

The barges and the bargees were always a nuisance, and the latter our natural enemies on the river. Generally there was one man in each barge; they were mostly coal-barges, rowed by two enormous sweeps – i.e. heavy oars – working on a sort of large thole-pin on each side, near the bows. The man leant on his sweeps and took two or three steps aft on the little deck in the bows of the barge, then leant backward and dragged them through.

The barges generally came drifting down on the tide, the man sometimes with one sweep out, giving a stroke from time to time to keep her head straight, but more often lolling up in the bows with a short black pipe in his mouth, and using filthy language to every boat that passed. They could not get out of your way if they tried. In this way they floated from bridge to bridge, but when they neared one they had to stand by their sweeps and steer for an arch. This required much care, and knowledge of the set of the tide, especially when nearing a bridge with partly-closed arches like Battersea, and for ten or fifteen minutes they could not leave their sweeps. In the old days – I speak of my father's time, about 1810 – the boys were always at war with them, and invented a very clever manner of annoying them. Boys, in a heavy funny, used to wait for a coal-barge just above a bridge. The bargee then had to take to his sweeps in the bows, to make his point for an arch. Then came the opportunity: the heavy funny was quickly moored to the stern of the barge, the boys jumped on board, and proceeded to pelt the bargee with his own coals.

If the bargee left his sweeps, he fouled the bridge, and the tormentors were quickly into their boat again and away.

This was told me by an old Westminster of 1811. I have always felt ashamed that we, in my time, had not sufficient invention to do likewise; the charging of Citizen steamers seems to have been invented in its place.

This required some care, and there was a little spice of danger about it that made it the more attractive. The time between forenoon school and dinner we often occupied in 'humbugging about' – i.e. general boating mischief. When we saw a penny steamboat coming down, we pulled across to her, and lay on our oars, with the bows of our heavy funny heading at right angles to her course. As soon as the paddles were abreast of us we gave way, and charged into her, trying to break the little bull's-eye cabin windows in her side. The captains used to object in choice lingo, but could not get at us, and we, though often a bit splashed by the swell from the paddles, always got safely away.

Capt. F. Markham, *Recollections of a Town Boy at Westminster*, 1903

Shakespeare's description of Cleopatra's barge in Antony and Cleopatra *sounds not unlike the craft used by the Lord Mayor and City dignitaries when it was the custom to make frequent Thames crossings between Westminster and Southwark. Enobarbus, friend to Antony, is talking to Agrippa and Mecaenas, Caesar's friends:*

ENOBARBUS. I will tell you.
   The barge she sat in, like a burnish'd throne,
   Burn'd on the water; the poop was beaten gold,
   Purple the sails, and so perfumed, that
   The winds were love-sick with them, the oars
      were silver,
   Which to the tune of flutes kept stroke, and
      made
   The water which they beat to follow faster,
   As amorous of their strokes. For her own person,
   It beggar'd all description; she did lie
   In her pavilion, – cloth-of-gold of tissue, –
   O'er-picturing that Venus where we see
   The fancy outwork nature; on each side her
   Stood pretty-dimpled boys, like smiling Cupids,
   With divers-colour'd fans, whose wind did seem
   To glow the delicate cheeks which they did cool,
   And what they undid did.
AGRIPPA.   O! rare for Antony.

ENOBARBUS. Her gentlewomen, like the Nereides,
  So many mermaids, tended her i' the eyes,
  And made their bends adornings; at the helm
  A seeming mermaid steers; the silken tackle
  Swell with the touches of those flower-soft hands,
  That yarely frame the office. From the barge
  A strange invisible perfume hits the sense
  Of the adjacent wharfs. The city cast
  Her people out upon her, and Antony,
  Enthron'd i' the market-place, did sit alone,
  Whistling to the air; which, but for vacancy,
  Had gone to gaze on Cleopatra too
  And made a gap in nature.
AGRIPPA.   Rare Egyptian!

William Shakespeare, *Antony and Cleopatra*, 1606–7

Charles Dickens described boating from Searle's yard in Lambeth :

What can be more amusing than Searle's yard on a fine Sunday morning? It's a Richmond tide, and some dozen boats are preparing for the reception of the parties who have engaged them. Two or three fellows in great rough trousers and Guernsey shirts, are getting them ready by easy stages; now coming down the yard with a pair of sculls and a cushion – then having a chat with the 'jack', who, like all his tribe, seems to be wholly incapable of doing anything but lounging about – then going back again, and returning with a rudder-line and a stretcher – then solacing themselves with another chat – and then wondering, with their hands in their capacious pockets, 'where them gentlemen's got to as ordered the six.' One of these, the head man, with the legs of his trousers carefully tucked up at the bottom, to admit the water, we presume – for it is an element in which he is infinitely more at home than on land – is quite a character, and shares with the defunct oysterswallower the celebrated name of 'Dando'. Watch him, as taking a few minutes' respite from his toils, he negligently seats himself on the edge of a boat, and fans his broad bushy chest with a cap scarcely half so furry. Look at his magnificent, though reddish whiskers, and mark the somewhat native humour with which he 'chaffs' the boys and 'prentices, or cunningly gammons the gen'lm'n into the gift of a glass of gin, of which we verily believe he swallows in one day as much as any six ordinary men, without ever being one atom the worse for it.

But the party arrives, and Dando, relieved from his state of uncertainty, starts up into activity. They approach in full aquatic costume, with round blue jackets, striped shirts, and caps of all sizes and patterns . . .

This is the most amusing time to observe a regular Sunday water-party. There has evidently been up to this period no inconsiderable degree of boasting on everybody's part relative to his knowledge of navigation; the sight of the water rapidly cools their courage, and the air of self-denial with which each of them insists on somebody else's taking an oar, is perfectly delightful.

At length, after a great deal of changing and fidgeting, consequent upon the election of a stroke-oar: the inability of one gentleman to pull on this side, of another to pull on that, and of a third to pull at all, the boat's crew are seated. 'Shove her off!' cries the coxswain, who looks as easy and comfortable as if he were steering in the Bay of Biscay. The order is obeyed; the boat is immediately turned completely round, and proceeds towards Westminster Bridge, amidst such a splashing and struggling as never was seen before, except when the Royal George went down. 'Back wa'ater, sir,' shouts Dando, 'Back wa'ater, you sir, aft;' upon which everybody thinking he must be the individual referred to, they all back water, and back comes the boat, stern first, to the spot whence it started. 'Back water, you sir, aft; pull round, you sir, for'ad, can't you?' shouts Dando, in a frenzy of excitement. 'Pull round, Tom, can't you?' re-echoes one of the party. 'Tom an't for'ad,' replies another. 'Yes, he is,' cries a third; and the unfortunate young man, at the imminent risk of breaking a blood-vessel, pulls and pulls, until the head of the boat fairly lies in the direction of Vauxhall Bridge. 'That's right – now pull all on you!' shouts Dando again, adding, in an under-tone, to somebody by him, 'Blowed if hever I see sich a set of muffs!' and away jogs the boat in a zigzag direction, every one of the six oars dipping into the water at a different time; and the yard is once more clear, until the arrival of the next party.

Charles Dickens, *Sketches by 'Boz'*, 1836

The Boat Race, though not as old as Doggett's Coat and Badge, is the best-known Tideway race. Before the late-Victorian boom in competitive and team sports, rowing provided the punter with much of his excitement, and Boat Race day, without the benefit of radio or television, was a

*sort of Derby Day occasion. Martin Cobbett, notebook in
hand, was there for the Referee:*

Some old readers can recollect what being afloat on a
'Varsity Boat-race day was, with every paddle steamer
the Thames Company could spare in commission to go
up with the crews, or, if unable to stand so high a trial
as that, to do its best to be there or thereabouts. How
was it that most of them escaped shipwrecks and
burstings and blowings up, and we who took our
chances abroad were not drowned, smashed, burnt,
boiled, or converted into sausage-meat among the
machinery, like the poor chap who went to a down-river
fight, and was taken out of the engine-room a spoonful
at a time? There they were, the passenger boats, whose
captains did their steering by wireless telegraphy, a
sort of deaf and dumb finger talk, to a watchful nipper,
who translated orders, signalled from the bridge, to the
engineer; such despatches as 'back her,' 'stop her,'
'half a tarn a-starn,' 'go on a-'ed.' There they were,
each doing its best pretty much regardless of the other
or consequences, charging and fouling, and ramming
into the rest, and being done to likewise. I have been
one of a crowd conveyed on a solid wall of, say, eight
or nine steamers jammed sponson to sponson, going
straight full speed at a buttress of Hammersmith Bridge
with a certainty thrown in of the funnels being smashed
off before they could be lowered on top of the wedged-
in passengers. If you or your ship got in front you might
see some of the rowing. Most likely all you did see was
the mob of boats ahead, and at that were thankful
indeed when the expected arrived in the shape of an
easy, and the time came for the devoted crew to go
round collecting in spare moments afforded through
something's going wrong with the works. In those days
the captain appointed himself official stakeholder, and

charged a shilling in the pound for acting as such. You could get your pocket picked on most reasonable terms, and probably did if you displayed money, or looked like being worth 'going over', and had had a good day if you didn't stop a live spark or some sort of grit with your eye before the voyage was over.

Martin Cobbett, *Sporting Notions*, 1908

A Rower's Life · I

I like a sport where I can expect to . . .
A. Be seen on television.
B. Play professionally after college.
C. Endorse Lite Beer when I retire.
D. Sit on my ass and go backwards.

from a questionnaire in the Rudder, 1981

*When done well rowing or sculling looks elegant, graceful,
and easy. But a lot of physical and mental effort goes into
the attainment of perfection of the stroke and its repetition.
When it is done right it is an astonishing feeling, exhilaration whether winning or losing. This chapter follows the
mixed fortunes of those who try :*

High on a Norroway mountain's crown,
    By the head of the winding firth,
A pine tree, slender and straight and brown,
    Came with a crash to earth,
Felt the bite of the whirring steel,
    Sailed o'er the northern sea;
And they fashioned her sixty feet of keel
    From the heart of that noble tree.

They shipped the trunk of a cedar stout
    From over the western main;
And the saw teeth worried a broad plank out,
    And the broad plank kissed the plane.
And the plane swished on, till the quivering sheet
    Was delicate, smooth, and thin;
And the thin sheet curved in the smoky heat,
    And gave her a rounded skin.

Her four steel riggers on either side
  Were bred from the ores of Spain;
Her straps were made of a black bull's hide,
  That fed on the Pampas plain.
Her canvas covers an Antrim green
  Had bleached to a snow-white hue;
And lastly, to quicken the whole machine,
  They gave her an English crew.

R. H. Forster, from *The Eagle*, June 1899

If you can force your heart and nerve and sinew
To drive your legs long after they are done
And so row on when there is nothing in you
Except the will that says 'Now on';
If you can fill the unforgiving minute
With forty strokes, and let the boat full run,
Yours is the earth and everything that's in it.
And what's more you'll be an oar, my son.

Dermod St John Gogarty, with apologies to
Rudyard Kipling, 1931

*There is only one way to try out a single scull. and that
is to go it alone : Mr Verdant Green, a fictional novice
dreamt up by the Revd Edward Bradley, had the sort of
initiation experienced since by many, in general if not in
detail :*

The aquatic desires that were now burning in Mr
Verdant Green's breast could only be put out by the
water; and so to the river he next day went, and by
Charles Larkyns' advice, made his first essay in a tub
from Hall's. Being a complete novice with the oars,
our hero had no sooner pulled off his coat and given a
pull, than he succeeded in catching a tremendous
'crab', the effect of which was to throw him backwards,
and almost to upset the boat. Fortunately, however,

'tubs' recover their equilibrium almost as easily as tombolas, and *Sylph* did not belie its character; so the freshman again assumed a proper position and was shoved off with a boat-hook. At first he made some hopeless splashes in the stream, the only effect of which was to make the boat turn with a circular movement towards Folly Bridge; but Charles Larkyns at once came to the rescue with the simple but energetic compendium of boating instruction, 'Put your oar in deep, and bring it out with a jerk!'

Bearing this in mind, our hero's efforts met with well merited success; and he soon passed that mansion which, instead of cellars, appears to have an ingenious system of small rivers to thoroughly irrigate its foundations. One by one, too, he passed those houseboats which are more like the Noah's arks of toyshops than anything else, and sometimes contain quite as original a mixture of animal specimens. Warming with his exertions, Mr Verdant Green passed the University barge in great style, just as the eight were preparing to start; and though he was not able to 'feather his oars with skill and dexterity,' like the jolly young waterman in the song, yet his sleight-of-hand performances with them proved not only a source of great satisfaction to the crews on the river, but also to the promenaders on the shore. He left the Christ Church meadows far behind, and was beginning to feel slightly exhausted by his unwonted exertions, when he reached that bewildering part of the river termed 'the Gut'. So confusing were the intestine commotions of this gut, that, after passing a chequered existence as an aquatic shuttlecock, and being assailed with a slang-dictionary-full of opprobrious epithets, Mr Verdant Green caught another tremendous crab, and before he could recover himself, the 'tub' received a shock, and, with a loud cry of 'Boat ahead!' ringing in his ears, the University Eight passed over the place where he and the *Sylph* had so lately disported themselves. . . .

Cuthbert Bede (the Revd Edward Bradley),
The Adventures of an Oxford Freshman, 1853

Some women's colleges in the United States introduced their students to rowing for deportment and recreation rather than racing. The Director of Physical Education at Wellesley College explains:

Rowing – for girls, let us be sure to assume, as men are not expected to benefit by this treatise – may be divided into skiff or pleasure rowing, pure and simple, and crew rowing, which is, indeed, also a pleasure for those who delight in constantly being found fault with because they cannot do twenty-six things at the same time, although it is not by any means simple or a recreation in the same sense with skiff rowing.

The general principles of good oarsmanship . . . must be everywhere the same, I imagine, whether developed and applied with an exhaustive study of mechanics by a racing eight or modestly exploited by a seeker of pond-lilies. Perhaps the choice between skiff and crew rowing must be decided by one's love of scenery, as the skiff oarswoman can happily gaze on

the face of Nature while the crew oarswoman fixes her
eye on the neck of the girl in front . . .

The physical benefits which women derive from
rowing cannot be exaggerated, provided they are willing
to master the rudiments of the sport – for one must
strive for good form, deep breathing, strength of back
and chest, and wear no tight or stiff clothing about the
waist. Correct rowing induces an erect carriage and
finely poised head, a full chest and well-placed
shoulders. Incorrect rowing disturbs all harmony of
the figure. One can row one's self round-shouldered as
easily as erect!

Lucille Eaton Hill, Athletics and Out-door Sports for
Women, 1903

*Styles of rowing and developments in boat and equipment
design which affected them sometimes occurred simultaneously, sometimes independently, on each side of the
Atlantic. The Tynesiders claim the outrigger (after the
Greek galleys) and the keel-less racing boat, the Americans
claim the sliding seat and the swivel rowlock for the oar.
The English claim the sliding foot-stretcher and rigger
which has had a German-inspired revival of interest in the
1980s. The Americans invented the paper sculling boat,
and here is how Charles Courtney, self-taught waterman
of Union Springs, New York State, encountered such an
unheard-of thing in 1868. He later became a renowned
coach of Cornell University:*

Even while building houses [Charles Courtney] was
accustomed in the evening and at other odd moments
to paddle around in the old Rob Roy which he and
Cozzens had built. One evening, while these two were
sitting in the back room of the Post Office, talking about
nothing in particular, one of their acquaintances, Noyes
Collins by name, walked in and sat down, remarking as
he did so,

'Say, Charley, I saw in the papers today that they have made a boat out of paper, twelve inches wide and thirty feet long.'

Charley replied, 'Noyes, they must be crazy,' and they all laughed at the idea.

'But anyway, it's so,' Noyes added, 'and a fellow named Tyler is going to row a race in her, if any one will compete with him.'

Then Cozzens said, 'Charley, let's put oars on our boat; we can find some lumber right here in Union Springs and make them ourselves.'

No sooner said than done, and a few days after the oars had been completed and tried out, notice came that a single scull race was advertised to take place at Aurora on a certain date. Everybody at once took it up and all were determined that [Charley] should go in; and so, says Charley, 'I finally consented to go, as I thought the Rob Roy, with her new oars, was about the finest and swiftest boat in the world. The big boats and yachts all went ahead, and I took the little craft in the steamer the next morning. Shall I ever forget the expression on the boys' faces when I met them on the dock at Aurora? Collins had a face about a mile long, and he exclaimed to me in a hoarse whisper, "My God, there's two men here with those shell boats, and you never saw such freakish-looking crafts in your life!"

'You have heard of people's hearts going down into their boots. When I went over into the storehouse with Collins, and saw those boats like two bars of polished steel – twelve inches wide and finished as beautifully as a piano body, I said, "Let's go and cover my boat up!" I had taken her from the steamer and put her out on Captain Angel's sail-boat, and she was quite a curiosity to the crowd, – a home-made craft in every sense of the word. Some city youths were standing around her, poking each other in the ribs, and giving sly winks, and I was just as ashamed of her as I could be. She weighed at least eighty pounds, which was probably twenty pounds more than the other two put together.

'Well the race was called at about three o'clock in the afternoon. The excitement was up to fever heat. Those two racing shells from New York were a complete surprise to everybody. As for me, I don't suppose I shall ever be able to describe the feelings and sensations that came over me when I took my position between them. There were looks of pity in the faces of my friends; they wanted to see me win, of course, but no one thought I had the ghost of a show. W. H. Bogart, of Aurora, started the race, and when I sat there waiting for the word, I realized that I was in a boat and I was out there to pull as I had never pulled before.

'But if those shell boats were a surprise, that race was a bigger one. Of course, my opponents were no good as oarsmen, or I never could have beaten them, but I just literally ran away from them. Much to their disgust and to the delight of the crowd, I crossed the line when they were still desperately trudging along somewhere down the course, and my first race was won. I think more of the little cup that was given to me as the prize on that occasion than any prize I have ever won.'

Charles Van Patten Young, *Courtney and Cornel'*
Rowing, 1923

Sliding seats arrived in the 1870s and because they afforded longer sweeps through the water with the blade, turned the advantage for effective rowing from the squat broad athlete capable of heaving short strokes at a high rate to the long-limbed who could take long strokes. Before the mechanical slide, however, came ingenious attempts to lengthen the stroke through sliding, by greasing one's shorts, or less drastic measures:

With the exception of the sculling boats, all boats had fixed pins, and this rig was not discarded until well into the Fifties; all the 'fours' had fixed seats: virtually only the 1st and 2nd Eights ever experienced the luxury of rowing on slides. But the fixed seats were not used altogether as such. Boys were encouraged to fortify their bottoms with thick sweaters and then to slide that small amount that a fixed seat permitted.

R. D. Hole, *Monkton Combe School Boat Club*, 1978

Forming an eight is a subject of endless controversy. St Paul's Magazine *attempted to explain the mysteries of captaincy to a foreigner in 1867. The editor who commissioned the piece was the novelist Anthony Trollope, and the writer was the Revd Leslie Stephen, a rower, writer, and alpinist of immense distinction. He later became editor of the* Cornhill Magazine *and the* Dictionary of National Biography, *after having relinquished orders. But there is no evidence that he broke faith with rowing:*

A captain requires as much skill in composing a crew as a minister in forming his cabinet . . . As in the larger world, each man chosen is apt to make one grumbler at his selection and half a dozen grumblers at their exclusion; and the mere task of keeping eight men in good temper who are all in a feverish state of hard work and excitement, and who have to take all their meals and pass most of their vacant hours in each other's company, is itself enough to try an angel.

Bow is an unpopular man, and ill-natured people maintain that he has been put in out of favouritism. Two takes the captain aside every other morning to reveal to him, – not without gloomy satisfaction, – a sure symptom of some new and fatal disease which he has just detected in a vital organ. Three is a picture of health and strength, but is so clumsy that no one knows whether he can be licked into tolerable shape in time. Four is a heavy good-tempered giant, who serves the invaluable purpose of being a butt to the rest of the crew at feeding times, but he is apt to lose his head, and then he is about as dangerous in a boat as a startled elephant in a caravan. Five would be unimpeachable, but for dark hints that he has a private score at some unknown public-house. Six labours under a chronic grievance, declaring with much loss of good temper to all his fellows that Four does not take his share of the work. Seven is really delicate, as Two professes to be, and will conceal his ailments till it is too late to find a substitute. And if the captain does not himself row, Stroke probably considers himself to be the one man in the University who understands the art of rowing, and has to be coaxed and wheedled into a decent subordination. The coxswain has been chosen after long deliberation on the ground that it is worth securing an ounce more brains at a cost of a stone more flesh, and all the crew are profoundly convinced that if they lose it will be owing to that superfluous weight in the stern-sheets.

Then there are perplexities about the boat, about the details of the work, about the cruel examiners who will torture some members of the crew, about the food supplied, and about a hundred other matters which are a constant tax upon the unlucky captain's fund of good humour. In short, a captain . . . is a man, who has to put together a complex machine formed of human beings; he has to choose it properly in the first instance, to adjust all its parts to each other, to keep it in good temper and due subordination, to prevent its stomachs from getting out of order or its muscles from growing flabby, and generally to devote to this compound Frankenstein an amount of time and attention which would almost entitle him to preside over an episcopal synod. Many races have been lost from the weakness of the crew, from the badness of the ship, from ill-luck in the start, and from a hundred other causes; but the one great and irremediable defect is a want of brains.

St Paul's Magazine, 1867

Clubs formed their own rules for training and diet; often sensible, sometimes bizarre. Here are Durham University's in 1884:

N.B. – Gentlemen are on their honour to keep these rules.

Rise at 7, or not later than 7.30. Cold bath and short walk or run before breakfast (about a mile).

Breakfast (8 o'clock). – Chops, steaks, cold meat (beef or mutton); bread as stale as possible – better toast – the less butter the better; eggs, watercress; tea (no coffee), not more than two ordinary breakfast cups.

Lunch. – A little cold meat (not necessary), bread and butter, and half a pint of beer.

Dinner. – Roast beef or mutton, fish or fowl in small quantities, vegetables (very little potato or green food), no pastry, jelly, beer – one pint.

Dessert. – Oranges, wine – two glasses at most of port or claret – *not* sherry; *no cheese*.

Tea. – Two small cups at most.

Bed. – 10, or not later than 10.30.

NO SMOKING

Capt. A. A. Macfarlane-Grieve, *A History of Durham Rowing*, 1922

A Rower's Life · II

All ye whose style is Orthodox,
  Who nobly ply the oar
With a firm, columnar swinging
  As your fathers did before,
Who reach right out and drive it through
  With solid body-heave,
Sink ancient animosities
  And give a cheer for Steve!

We know that curious style of his
  Is most completely wrong;
But for all his leg-drive heresy
  His boats *do* get along!
It must be subtle wizardry,
  So, whatever we believe,
Here's to 'the best of coaches' –
  Come, give a cheer for Steve!

R. E. Swartwout, *Rhymes of the River*, 1927

Steve Fairbairn is known universally in the rowing world as Steve. He was an Australian coach who first took on his own college, Jesus, Cambridge, and then Thames and London rowing clubs and eventually spread his influence by correspondence throughout the world. He took on the English Orthodox style of rowing which owed its somewhat stiff and formal roots largely to Eton and Oxford. Steve believed that you should enjoy what you are doing, and to enjoy it you should be comfortable, not strait-jacketed, and that since a crew is only as strong as its weakest man you should do your very best for and with the material you

*have available, whatever their various shapes or sizes.
The controversy he caused about style started in 1900 and
continued long and bitterly after his death in 1938, and
still echoes across a river or lake occasionally. R. E.
Swartwout, a witty rhymester from the Cambridge
magazine* Granta, *introduces him above. Steve's coaching
hints will contribute occasionally to the debate hereafter,
but first a whisper from Oxford, the bastion of straight-
backed and tight-lipped Orthodoxy:*

My first days of 'tubbing' in a heavy clapboard, four-
oared contraption with fixed seats were directed by an
antique don who apparently had come out of the wood-
work. He wore a frayed, faded Leander cap, which
meant he must have been an old Blue, a trials man or
have rowed in a Head of the River boat . . . His instruction was, I gathered, faithful to the orthodoxy of Oxford
and Cambridge rowing, as developed at Eton, which
has always supplied the universities with good oarsmen.
Rowing, he explained, was an art in which the oar was
moved through the water by the legs and the swing of
the back: the arms were merely the connection of the
back with the oar. This made the 'English' method of
rowing a rhythmic movement of beauty.

He warned us that there was in being, in actual
practice, a deplorable heresy preached by a man named
Steve Fairbairn, an Australian, in which the back was
disregarded in its proper emphasis and the arms were
used to finish the stroke. This Australian had taught his
baleful ideas to the crews of Jesus College, Cambridge,
with the sad result that Jesus had gone Head of the
River on the Cam before the war. Fairbairn had also
taught the Jesus style to the Light Blue or Cambridge
Eight with disgustingly successful results. He had even
imparted his revolutionary ideas to a tideway rowing
club which had done depressingly well at Henley in

1914. Fairbairn was quoted by the old don as having said, 'It's better to go fast than look good!' The blasphemy was whispered to us.

Raymond Massey, in *My Oxford*, 1977

Showiness is not always evidence of usefulness. If one sees eight men carrying a coffin, four of them with backs bent under the load, and the other four turning their toes out like dancing-masters, one knows who is carrying the coffin.

Steve Fairbairn

The coach's best friend is the bicycle. The Sir Henry who is 'riding by sublime' in the piece that follows is Sir Henry Howard, a well-known Cambridge coach of the Twenties. 'Eyes in the boat' is part of the Orthodox creed and its command is guaranteed to draw attention to something on the bank:

> From age to age we change our ways;
>   We must turn History's course back
> If we would seek the nobler days
>   When coaches rode on horseback.
>
> Of course, we may at any time
>   Observe at our discretion
> Sir Henry riding by sublime,
>   Head of a proud procession;
>
> But riding prancing, snorting bays
>   Is not much to the liking
> Of those who coach in Lents or Mays –
>   They mostly stick to biking.
>
> O push-bike, what a help are you
>   In tow-path demonstrations,
> Explaining to each budding Blue
>   The coach's inculcations!

'Observe how with a *rapid* poke
   I keep this bike-wheel spinning;
That's what I mean, my worthy stroke,
   By getting the beginning.'

And if he has a proper lack
   Of feeling, he'll exclaim,
'Bow, the roundness of your back
   Would put this wheel to shame!'

A certain coach one time I knew
   Who was forever shouting,
'Eyes in the boat!' until his crew
   Dreaded the daily outing;

His really thoughtful two-wheeled steed
   Threw him, by Baitsbite Locks;
When he emerged, all mud and weed,
   'EYES IN THE BOAT!' cried cox.

           R. E. Swartwout, *Rhymes of the River*, 1927

Orthodoxy is particularly severe on keeping the eyes in the boat. This not only turns the body into cast-iron, but also paralyses the mind.

                                Steve Fairbairn

Dr Furnivall, whom we met earlier on his picnicking voyages, found a way of taking eight girls out together:

In 1904 the Doctor purchased from New College, Oxford, a best rowing eight, which was converted into a sculling eight for the use of the club. This boat created quite a sensation on the water-side when it was first launched, being the only sculling eight in existence, and the Doctor's great ambition was to have it out as often as possible. Many journeys to and from Richmond were performed, before the memorable occasion when it was manned by eight girls, with the Doctor as coxswain. This took place after a race between two girls' fours; the competing crews disembarked from the boats in which they had just raced and took their places in the eight. The trip performed was only a short one, but was sufficient to prove that the girls were capable of its management, and showed watermanship equal to any previous crew. This, needless to say, filled the Doctor with pride, and nothing would satisfy him but that they should appear again.

The next time they were afloat they were exposed to a battery of cameras belonging to the various newspaper reporters, with the result that photographs of the girls' eight and their president coxswain, together with articles by the latter, appeared in all the daily papers and weekly newspapers. By this means the girls' eight became quite world-famous. The Doctor claimed it as the only sculling eight, which caused the girls of an American college to send over illustrations of their eights; but their style proved to be rowing, and so the Doctor's contention was maintained.

Gwendoline Jarvis, *Memories of F. J. Furnivall*, 1911

There are frightening statistics leading to an elusive, but possible, goal:

In the average season an oarsman will race seven times for a total of about forty-four minutes. In preparation for that three quarters of an hour, he will train a total of 900 hours. All sports are demanding, but crew, unlike most, requires that the athlete train throughout the summer as well. Of these 900 hours, 600 will be spent running as many as twelve miles per day, lifting weights, cross-country skiing, and sprinting up and down stadium stairs. During the 300 hours on the water, he will take approximately 252,000 strokes. All this for forty-four minutes of competition. Add to this another 300 hours of showering and running to and from the boathouse, and one has plenty of reasons not to row . . .

There is a state of awareness achieved about the ninth mile of a twelve-mile run, where the upper body separates from the legs, and there is no pain, only the weird desire to keep running. There is the thrill in pounding out 100 hard strokes, using up all your energy, and then doing another 100-stroke drive and having it feel just as strong.

The oarsman is not a man alone. If his crew is to succeed he must become perfectly synchronized with the other men in the boat. Sometimes, for thirty or forty strokes – more if the crew is really good and well-matched – all men in the boat will move together. Every move the stroke makes will be mirrored by the men behind him, all the catches will hit hard and clean, like a trout going after a fly, and they will hit at precisely the same instant. When that happens, the boat begins to lift up off the water, air bubbles running under the bow, and there is an exhilaration like nothing else I have ever experienced. For the duration of the drive, everything else is effortless, and it is literally like flying.

Brad Brinegar, *Dartmouth Alumni Magazine*, June 1977

The best coach for any crew is the bows of a faster boat
coming behind them.

Steve Fairbairn

East Germany's obsession with sporting prowess has in-
cluded rowing. They win more than the rest, who fre-
quently snap at their heels with well-honed crews in
individual events. Here is their training manual discussing
The Sporting Personality:

The effects of the education should be fundamentally
that all sporting activities, all actions in training, every
technical or theoretical instruction and general daily
conduct must be bound together with the principles of
educational philosophy, the development of character
and will—in short to the development of a well-balanced
sporting personality. This is more easily said than done.
We can here put forward a few aims and methods:

1. First of all an opening of the personality, pleasure
in rowing, and enthusiasm are to be developed, via
experiences of success and an interesting and varied
training. The beginner especially counts every problem
which he can satisfactorily solve as a successful experience.

2. Discussions over important current affairs, both
national and sporting, are amongst the most important
tasks within a rowing group.

3. Order, cleanliness, punctuality and disciplined
behaviour corresponding to the order within the boathouse must be demanded and monitored until they have
become a natural characteristic of the oarsman.

4. The ability to work hard in training and to be a
reliable member of a crew, are best developed by
membership of a firm crew, drawing on mutual education under the 'invisible' lead of the coach or trainer.

5. A sense of responsibility will be strengthened if each oarsman is given a task for the crew, for the boathouse, or for the club.

6. The sportsman must be encouraged to think and act for himself, so that in training and above all when racing correct decisions can be made. Fairbairn used to say that one should coach in such a way that the person being coached can coach himself. The coach is not a nursemaid!

7. The desire to achieve good performances, to overcome weaknesses and to reach the target must become the personal leading motive of the oarsman, via the coach's demands. In the end, the coach's demands and the desires of the oarsman must coincide.

8. The relationship of trust between sportsman and coach is a prerequisite of satisfactory development. It is established first of all by correct actions, solid behaviour, and critical analysis of mistakes, and by friendly help extending to questions of private life.

9. The coach or leader is also responsible for seeing that despite heavy training loads, performance in school, or similar is kept at a high level. (Organize daily routine!)

10. A sensible use of free time in the boathouse, friendly moral relationships with the opposite sex, and mutual readiness to help should be taken for granted. The coach must watch, lead, and criticize helpfully.

11. The growth and development of the educational process is the greater and longer-lasting if the coach can succeed in getting the parents, youth organization, functionaries of the club, and the pupil's own comrades into the front line.

Dr Ernst Herberger and others, German Democratic Republic's textbook of rowing (trans. John. Langfield with Bruce Grainger), 1974

The only time to speak to an individual is when he shows improvement.

Steve Fairbairn

The oarsman has ways of dealing with the coach who gets too heavy:

Get in smartly! To ensure this, depress the handle of the oar as far as possible. This will raise the blade several feet above the water; look curiously at it, and, at any moment convenient to yourself, bring it down with a splash.

Don't do too much work; the rest of the crew will do it, and you will thus have plenty left in you for the spurt at the finish.

Never let your eyes leave the blade of your oar; you never know what it may do if not watched.

Make a point of advising your cox, on all occasions of emergency; he enjoys having several opinions to choose from.

If possible, wear 'footer' jerseys; it emphasizes the fact that rowing is not your only accomplishment.

Don't watch the man in front of you; it detracts from the attention necessary for your oar, and in any case he has no more right to dictate than anyone else.

If you get in late, say nothing worth recording, but correct the error by getting in too soon next stroke.

When you see an opportunity of getting in two strokes to stroke's one, seize it, it always proves a welcome diversion.

In conclusion, avoid machine-like regularity; nothing is so offensive as a crew that shows a lack of individuality.

Durham University Journal, 1900

A volume of good rowing poetry would be a slim one indeed; but a collection of entertaining songs, rhymes, couplets, and ditties would add up to a chunky little work. Popular songs and undergraduate sheets are the ideal places for the bards to find space to muse. Rudie Lehmann, (1856–1929) founder of Cambridge's Granta, *staff-writer at* Punch, *and coach of some renown, was a master in the genre. Here is part of his 'The Perfect Oar', or what everyone should be driving at :*

His hands are ever light to catch;
  Their swiftness is astounding;
No billiard ball could pass or match
  The pace of their rebounding.
Then, joyfully released and gay,
  And graceful as Apollo's,
With what a fine columnar sway
  His balanced body follows!

He keeps his sturdy legs applied
  Just where he has been taught to,
And always moves his happy slide
  Precisely as he ought to.

He owns a wealth of symmetry
  Which nothing can diminish,
And strong men shout for joy to see
  His wonder-working finish.

He never rows his stroke in dabs –
  A fatal form of sinning –
And never either catches crabs
  Or misses the beginning.
Against his ship the storm winds blow,
  And every lipper frets her:
He hears the cox cry, 'Let her go!'
  And swings and drives and lets her.

Besides, he has about his knees,
  His feet, his wrists, his shoulders,
Some points which make him work with ease
  And fascinate beholders,
He is, in short, impeccable,
  And – this perhaps is oddest
In one who rows and looks so well –
  He is supremely modest.

He always keeps his language cool,
  Nor stimulates its vigour
In face of some restrictive rule
  Of dietary rigour.
And when the other men annoy
  With trivial reproaches,
He is the Captain's constant joy,
  The comfort of his coaches.

When grumblers call the rowing vile,
  Or growl about the weather,
Our Phoenix smiles a cheerful smile
  And keeps the crew together.

No 'Hump' is his – when everything
  Looks black his zeal grows stronger,
And makes his temper, like his swing,
  Proportionately longer.

One aim is his through weeks of stress –
  By each stroke rowed to aid work.
No facile sugared prettiness
  Impairs his swirling blade-work.
And oh, it makes the pulses go
  A thousand to the minute
To see the man sit down and row
  A ding-dong race and win it!

The College Bumps

Once, my dear, – but the world was young, then –
  Magdalen elms and Trinity limes –
Lissom the blades and the backs that swung then,
  Eight good men in the good old times –
Careless we, and the chorus flung then
  Under St Mary's chimes!

Sir Arthur Quiller-Couch, 'Alma Mater',
Oxford Magazine, 1896

From gaining a Blue in the Boat Race to joining the rugby
club's crew for a lowly division of the bumps, rowing has
been a popular pastime at both Oxford and Cambridge
since the boys of Eton and Westminster introduced their
sport to the ancient universities in the early nineteenth
century. There are a lot more rowing schools now, and in
any case novices can be recruited at any age. But not all
the recruits find the Oxbridge way of rowing attractive :

I had come from a rowing school. Situated as it was in
lush council surroundings, School (as the jargon had it)
lay no more than half a mile from Oaklands Park, that
stretch of rolling chickweed which separates Foskett
Bros (Grocers) Ltd from Standard Telephone & Cable,
in verdant North London. Each summer afternoon, we
day boys – the school being co-educational, many
senior couples were given to spending the night in the
bicycle shed – would stroll across to the park and buy
such hours of boating as the fruits of our mugging
would allow.

In consequence of this regular training, I became
something of an oar, able quite often to keep both

blades in the water simultaneously; and it was therefore only natural that my thoughts turned to the Oxford boat.

It was even more natural, after my first glimpse of the river, that they turned away again. There, in the chill fog, hundreds of young men paddled about in their underwear, their skin tripe-dimpled, their teeth leaving on the icy air the impression of a Flamenco eisteddfod. I, who had never touched oar without first buttoning my herringbone overcoat tightly about me, was shocked: no beer-crates cheered their skinny water-logged shells, no gramophones sang at their sterns, no busts broke the heaving vertical contours! This was not rowing as we that love the true sport know it.

Alan Coren, from *My Oxford*, 1977

Bump races developed independently at Oxford and Cambridge. Crews are started in divisions, there being racing on several days. If a crew is bumped by the one behind, or in some cases overlapped by them, they start in a lower position on the following day, and the crew who finish up at the top of the first division are Head of the River. Other rituals are attached to the bumps, such as bump suppers to celebrate upward progress in the divisions. The races are held twice a year, known as the Lent and May races at Cambridge and the Torpids and Eights at Oxford, and are central to the rowing life of the colleges. Most rowing centres in Britain now run Head of the River races between the onset of autumn and the spring. These are like bumping races without the bumps, being time trials raced in procession. The Head races were developed to make winter training more entertaining; the Oxbridge bumps, though, have always had a touch of romance and spectator appeal:

Shortly after this, the rest of us agreed it was time to be gone. We walked along the fields past the church, crossed the boat-house ferry, and mingled with the crowd upon the opposite bank. Townsmen and Gownsmen, with the laced Fellow-commoner sprinkled among them here and there – reading men and sporting men – Fellows, and even Masters of Colleges, not indifferent to the prowess of their respective crews – all these, conversing on all topics, from the slang in Bell's Life to the last new German Revelation, and moving in ever-changing groups down the banks, where, at the farthest visible bend of the river, was a little knot of ladies gathered upon a green knoll, faced and illuminated by the beams of the setting sun. Beyond which point was heard at length some indistinct shouting, which gradually increased, until 'They are off – they are coming!' suspended other conversation among ourselves: and suddenly the head of the first boat turned the corner, and then another close upon it, and then a third; the crews pulling with all their might, but in perfect rhythm and order; and the crowd upon the bank turning round to follow along with them, cheering, 'Bravo, St John's,' 'Go it, Trinity,' and waving hats and caps – the high crest and blowing forelock of Phidippus's mare, and he himself shouting encouragement to his crew, conspicuous over all – until, the boats reaching us, we also were caught up in the returning tide of spectators, and hurried back toward the boat-house; where we arrived just in time to see the ensign of Trinity lowered from its pride of place, and the eagle of St John's soaring there instead. Then, waiting a while to hear how it was the winner had won, and the loser had lost, and watching Phidippus engaged in eager conversation with his defeated brethren, I took Euphranor and Lexilogus, one under each arm (Lycion having strayed into better company elsewhere), and walked home with them across the meadow that lies between the river and the town, whither the dusky troops of gownsmen were evaporating, while twilight gathered over all, and the nightingale began to be heard among the flowering chestnuts of Jesus.

Edward Fitzgerald, *Euphranor*, 1851

After school at Rugby Tom Brown found himself rowing for his Oxford college, according to Thomas Hughes's heavy-handed sequel to the moralizing delights of Tom Brown's Schooldays. *Here, in one of the best passages, he describes St Ambrose's first bump:*

There it comes, at last – the flash of the starting gun. Long before the sound of the report can roll up the river, the whole pent-up life and energy which has been held in leash, as it were, for the last six minutes, is let loose, and breaks away with a bound and a dash which he who has felt it will remember for his life, but the like of which, will he ever feel again? The starting ropes drop from the coxswains' hands, the oars flash into the water, and gleam on the feather, the spray flies from them, and the boats leap forward . . .

For the first ten strokes Tom was in too great fear of making a mistake to feel or hear or see. His whole soul was glued to the back of the man before him, his one thought to keep time, and get his strength into the stroke. But as the crew settled down into the well-known long sweep, what we may call consciousness returned; and while every muscle in his body was straining, and his chest heaved, and his heart leapt, every nerve seemed to be gathering new life, and his senses to wake into unwonted acuteness. He caught the scent of the wild thyme in the air, and found room in his brain to wonder how it could have got there, as he had never seen the plant near the river, or smelt it before. Though his eye never wandered from the back of Diogenes, he seemed to see all things at once. The boat behind, which seemed to be gaining – it was all he could do to prevent himself from quickening on the stroke as he fancied that – the eager face of Miller [the coxswain], with his compressed lips, and eyes fixed so earnestly ahead that Tom could almost feel the glance passing over his right shoulder; the flying banks and the shouting crowd . . .

But it can't last for ever; men's muscles are not steel, or their lungs bull's hide, and hearts can't go on pumping a hundred miles an hour long without bursting. The St Ambrose boat is well away from the boat behind, there is a great gap between the accompanying crowds; and now, as they near the Gut, she hangs for a moment or two in hand, though the roar from the bank grows louder and louder, and Tom is already aware that the St Ambrose crowd is melting into the one ahead of them.

'We must be close to Exeter!' The thought flashes into him, and it would seem into the rest of the crew at the same moment. For, all at once, the strain seems taken off their arms again; there is no more drag; she springs to the stroke as she did at the start; and Miller's face, which had darkened for a few seconds, lightens up again . . . The water rushes by, still eddying from the strokes of the boat ahead. Tom fancies now he can hear their oars and the workings of their rudder, and the voice of their coxswain ... Then Miller, motionless as a statue till now, lifts his right hand and whirls the tassel round his head: 'Give it her now, boys; six strokes and we're into them.' Old Jervis lays down that great broad back, and lashes his oar through the water with the might of a giant, the crew catch him up in another stroke, the tight new boat answers to the spurt, and Tom feels a little shock behind him, and then a grating sound, as Miller shouts, 'Unship oars bow and three,' and the nose of the St Ambrose boat glides quietly up the side of the Exeter, till it touches their stroke oar.

Thomas Hughes, *Tom Brown at Oxford*, 1861

The passage to the Head of the River is laden with obstacles, not least the mischief of Eros on the bank. Zuleika Dobson, niece of the warden of Judas College, Oxford, was 'making an impression' on the young men about her according to Max Beerbohm's account of the femme fatale's *visit to the Summer Eights in 1911 :*

The Judas Eight had just embarked for their voyage to the starting-point. Standing on the edge of the raft that makes a floating platform for the barge, William, the hoary bargee, was pushing them off with his boathook, wishing them luck with deferential familiarity. The raft was thronged with old Judasians – mostly clergymen – who were shouting hearty hortations, and evidently trying not to appear so old as they felt – or rather, not to appear so startlingly old as their contemporaries looked to them. ...

The enormous eight young men in the thread-like skiff – the skiff that would scarce have seemed an adequate vehicle for the tiny 'cox' who sat facing them – were staring up at Zuleika with that uniformity of impulse which, in another direction, had enabled them to bump a boat on two of the previous 'nights'. If tonight they bumped the next boat, Univ., then would

Judas be three places 'up' on the river; and tomorrow Judas would have a Bump Supper. Furthermore, if Univ. were bumped tonight, Magdalen might be bumped tomorrow. Then would Judas, for the first time in history, be head of the river. Oh tremulous hope! Yet, for the moment, these eight young men seemed to have forgotten the awful responsibility that rested on their over-developed shoulders. Their hearts, already strained by rowing, had been transfixed this afternoon by Eros' darts. All of them had seen Zuleika as she came down to the river; and now they sat gaping up at her, fumbling with their oars. The tiny cox gaped too; but it was he who first recalled duty. With piping adjurations he brought the giants back to their senses. The boat moved away down stream, with a fairly steady stroke.

Not in a day can the traditions of Oxford be sent spinning. From all the barges the usual punt-loads of young men were being ferried across to the towing-path – young men naked of knee, armed with rattles, post-horns, motor-hooters, gongs, and other instruments of clangour. Though Zuleika filled their thoughts, they hurried along the towing-path, as by custom, to the starting-point.

Max Beerbohm, *Zuleika Dobson*, 1911

In its early days rowing was a great calling for men of the cloth, perhaps only because there were proportionately more of them roaming the groves of academe then than there are in the late-twentieth century. For example, St John's College, Cambridge, whose boat club is known as Lady Margaret after one of their earliest craft, claims from its crews for 1828–30 two bishops, a dean, the chaplain to Canton, three canons, a chaplain to the House of Commons, two rural deans and two surrogates, as well as a host of senior lawyers, scholars of Hebrew through to Divinity, and fifty-nine college prizewinners. They kept their heads clear by winning forty-one out of fifty-five races during the period. Certainly rowers regard their sport as a religion even if they differ about creeds :

Sir, 'Throughout his life my father remained a sportsman in the best sense of that painful word. After supper with three Pembroke colleagues on the eve of the Coxswainless fours, a pious member of the crew suggested that all should kneel and offer a silent word to the only sure source of victory. "Hang it", said my father, already an ordinand, "we mustn't take an unfair advantage of them".' – Sir Ronald Storrs in his autobiography *Orientations*, page 3.

Yours etc,

G. HENRY TALLACK.

Letter in *The Times*, 11 May 1981

He saw the dark wainscot and timbered roof,
    The long tables, and the faces merry and keen;
The College Eight and their trainer dining aloof,
    The Dons on the dais serene.

Henry Newbolt (1862–1938), 'He Fell among Thieves'

A major function of the college captains at Oxford and Cambridge is to elect the President of the respective University Boat Club and provide him with enough good men and true to form a Blue boat to defend or challenge in the Boat Race. As the senior sport, rowing's adherents have often appeared arrogant and unacademic. Henry Newbolt's lines above are the thoughts of a man waiting death by the sword somewhere near Afghanistan and show the place of the crew in the scheme of things. What follows is a more recent observation which shows an unacceptable face of the sport:

At Oxford there was a separate table in college hall where the first eight sat down to porterhouse steak and porter, and was not everyone else allowed to know it? 'Bloody hell, man', one heard resounding across the junior common room on some point of non-rowing issue. 'I *am* president of the OUBC.' Tradition had taught oarsmen to feel different, privileged perhaps, and Henley has never done anything to dissuade them.

Jeremy Alexander, *The Field*, 1981

Presidents could fall in unexpected ways, witness Dukker McLean's meeting with Desdemona in the mid-1880s as reported by Theodore Cook when he was in Oxford trying for a scholarship from Radley:

I did not win a scholarship that time. Even my evenings, sad to relate, were not as quiet as might have been wished. Benson had brought one of his companies down, at that time, to act Othello in the old theatre; and Miss Featherstonhaugh as Desdemona was so ravishingly beautiful that when she was smothered in her night-gown an audible shudder went through all the spectators, and a tall man in front of me stood up suddenly and fainted. It was D. H. McLean, then President of the Oxford University Boat Club, as I recognized when he was being taken out into the fresh air and a small undergraduate followed the procession carrying his gold spectacles. I hope the curtain had by then descended, for I am sure nobody looked at anything except 'Dukker'.

T. A. Cook, *The Sunlit Hours*, 1925

The Boat Race was immortalized by the wireless broadcasts of John Snagge and now has millions of spectators by courtesy of the BBC's television coverage. But it started long before broadcasting, at Henley in 1829, and moved to the Tideway for the second race in 1836. Here is an account of the first meeting:

The 'iron horse' was but in its infancy, and the 'road' was still in its glory, when Henley on that memorable Wednesday, the 10th of June 1829, first woke to the echoes of University cheers. Though boat-racing had not then the hold upon the public mind which it now boasts, Oxonians turned out on that day in far greater numbers than we see even in these days. All available hacks and traps in Oxford were requisitioned. Through Bensington, down the steeps of Nettlebed Hill, and along the 'Fair Mile', came tandems, drags, and saddle horses in strings. Cantabs also were there in force, though hardly in such numbers as their rivals, for the distance from headquarters was greater. The course

selected was from Hambleden Lock to Henley Bridge, $2\frac{1}{4}$ miles against a summer stream ... The Oxford colours were modelled upon those of Christ Church, then head of the river, who contributed four men and the coxswain to the Oxford boat. The Cambridge crew rowed in their white shirts, with a light pink sash. There were three Trinity men in the boat, and three of Lady Margaret, then head of the river. The uniform of the former was a buff jersey with blue stripes, of the latter a white jersey with light pink stripes. The crew could not agree which to wear, so they finally decided to row in their shirts, each man wearing a pink tie or sash in compliment to the captain, Snow, who was a Lady Margaret man.

The evening was warm and sunny. Those who have seen Henley on a fine summer's evening, a real old-fashioned summer, now, like the noble elms on Regatta Island, a cherished memory, can picture to themselves the scene, the wood-crowned hills surrounding the rich pasture land, the broad silver reach of the river, the fine old grey stone bridge, the square church tower, familiar landmark to many generations of keen-eyed coxswains, and the historical poplars, veritable *metae sudantes* of struggling oarsmen, now, like many of those who rowed past them, gone to make room for a progenium not, let us hope, *vitiosiorem*. The river below the island lies in a curve; but from Hambleden Lock there is a straight course up stream of nearly one hundred yards. Cambridge won the toss for choice of sides, and chose the tow-path, or Berks shore. They were the favourites in public estimation, especially when it became known that they had won the choice of stations. Each side nominated its own umpire, the two umpires to fix upon a referee if they should be unable to agree. . . . Never was the soundness of the doctrine of muscular Christianity more happily exemplified. . . . Two Bishops, three Deans, a Prebendary, and other clerical and legal dignitaries are an unusually high percentage to expect from any eighteen University men selected at hazard! . . .

The result of the race of that day is a matter of history. Oxford carried off the first '*corona navalis*' in University races. There was a foul soon after starting, but the boats returned to their stations, and recommenced the race. Then Oxford drew well away, and came by the island with a clear lead. From this point their superior strength told, and they swung up the time-honoured reach with a length well in hand, winning at the bridge by five or six lengths. The time is variously recorded from 11 min. to 14 min. 10 secs. No doubt the latter is approximately correct. Until outriggers came into vogue, the Henley course proper – from island to bridge – was never rowed under 8 min. Great was the hurly-burly when the race was over . . . 'Such a getting home agin' down Nettlebed Hill was never seen; yet those who were there to see do not tell us that any limbs were broken, or that the proctors made themselves obnoxious.

George Treherne and J. H. D. Goldie,
The Record of the University Boat Race, 1884

Rudder Strings

When Peaceful Edgar ruled the land
    He had eight kings at his command;
How did he tame this royal band?
    Ah, he was knowing!
These kings he did not subjugate
And make them draw his coach of state
Like Tamburlaine; he built an eight
    And taught them rowing.

R. E. Swartwout, Rhymes of the River, 1927

*Naturally Edgar the Peaceful took the steersman's seat.
'Cox,' warned Steve Fairbairn in one of his thoughts for
the day, 'is too often overlooked. He is almost the most
important man in the boat.' There are certainly occasions
when a coxswain can lose a race for a crew by bad or
ignorant steering, and once in a blue moon he or she can
win a race by doing the right thing at the right time.
Coxswains are a species unto themselves:*

It has been said that a tenor is not a man but a disease.
Similarly it may be said of coxswains that they are not
so much individual men as members of a tribe or secret
society formed entirely of male human beings weighing
on an average eight stone. They have meeting-places
where they come together to devise the torments which
later on they inflict on their fellow-mortals. They have
signs and passwords. One coxswain recognizes the
approach of another long before ordinary burly men
are aware of it. You may see the little creature cock up

his head while his eyes assume a tense look and his body quivers with excitement . . .

R. C. Lehmann, Sportsmen and Others, 1912

Sue Brown became the first woman to steer the men's Boat Race in 1981, but women have been taking the back seat for longer than they have pulled oars themselves. Height is not generally an asset for a cox whose role does not include that of wind-break or sail if it can be avoided. But it is obviously an advantage in some places such as the busy shipping lanes of Calcutta, at this time a watering place for clippers:

Mrs Daniell was most successful as a coxswain, her extraordinary height enabling her to look clear over the head of the bow oar in an 'eight', while her knowledge of the river and her able manipulation of the rudder lines made her services much prized.

L. H. Macklin, A Summary of the Records of the
Calcutta Rowing Club 1858–1932

Coxswains need respect, cheek, and low cunning. They are also, by definition, deaf:

Coxswains, like white cats with blue eyes are always deaf – at least during the earlier years of their professional career; and sometimes they remain deaf to the very end. Have you ever heard a coach endeavouring to cause his crew to cease rowing? Etiquette forbids him to do this by shouting directly to his men: he is compelled to use the coxswain as an intermediary. This is how it goes:

COACH [*to his crew*]. 'Now, then, we'll row about two hundred yards hard, and then easy. I'll start you. Get ready! Forward all! Are you ready? Row!'

[*The crew starts with the usual amount of splashing, No. 5 missing the water altogether and coming off his sliding seat.*]

[71]

COACH [*at top of voice*]. 'Oh, that won't do! That's awful! Easy, Cox!' [*Cox says nothing.*] 'EASY, COX!' [*The Cox sits tight, and utters no sound. The Coach becomes purple with passion, and begins to howl like a menagerie. At last the crew takes the matter into its own hands, and somehow a stoppage is brought about.*]

COACH [*in a tone of cold and cutting irony*]. 'Cox, if you would do me the extreme favour of trying, merely *trying*, to listen to what I say, it is just within the bounds of possibility that the crew would get on better. Personally I should prefer *not* to have to shout to you fifteen times. Now, then, we'll try another start.'

[*This time the Coxswain eases the crew long before the Coach meant it to stop, and so the game goes on.*]

R. C. Lehmann, *Sportsmen and Others*, 1912

Controlling a sixty-foot frail galley on a narrow bendy river with a stroppy crew and cantankerous coach is not always a pleasure cruise. The experienced cox, however, becomes the right-hand man of the coach, picking up his vibrations and the faults of the rowers and trying to reconcile them. Between the pair of them, coach and cox can have a rare old roundel:

I

Ahead, scul-lar!
  The deaf old ox –
Yes, easy cox.

'Hi, where's your mar!'
  The bargee mocks;
Ahead, scul-lar!
  The deaf old ox!

The rest I bar –
   The language shocks
The orthodox.
   Ahead, scul-lar!
The deaf old ox!
   Yes, easy, cox!

II

Your stroke's eighteen –
   Now, harder back,
It's getting slack!
The worst I've seen!
   A lazy pack.
Your stroke's eighteen –
   Now, harder back,

And finish clean,
   You're like a sack –
It's guts you lack.
   Your stroke's eighteen –
Now, harder back!
   It's getting slack!

III

Now, sit the boat!
   Don't flop about,
But steady out!

The worst afloat
   Without a doubt –
Now, sit the boat,
   Don't flop about.

BOATING

One needs a throat
  Of brass to shout
At such a lout –
  Now, sit the boat!
Don't flop about,
  But steady out!

R. E. Swartwout, *Rhymes of the River*, 1927

Henley

I spent happy hours on the Isis, but the best was Henley. There we were in competition with the finest crews of several nationalities, and at no moment in my life have I experienced so *sustained* a wish to excel. For those few days we lived in dread of the next race, discussing tactics, grooming the boat, eating enormously, sleeping long – and then the last terrified backward glance at the course before the race began in distant privacy to end ten minutes later between banks of parasols and tumultuous acclaim. Those were ecstatic moments.

Nigel Nicolson, from My Oxford, 1977

Henley Royal Regatta has always been a showcase of English rowing. Until the Second World War it was a bastion of the sort of amateurism which put people who worked with their hands beyond the Pale, but now it encompasses most aspects of British rowing. Since the turn of the century it has been a major battlefield between the English and foreigners, particularly Americans. It keeps its own oligarchical counsel and its own rules but cautiously keeps up with change in the sport, and thrives. Everybody loves Henley even if they hate it, and if, like Nigel Nicolson above, you get the added pleasure of earning a place there with a crew, and experience there the elusive ecstasy which all oarsmen seek, then you have found heaven on earth:

Henley Regatta, for a sequence of years unbroken, thirty long, not counting more ancient history, has been your humble servant's holiday-making first choice in

all the whole year's diversions. A big extra dose of
pleasure I extract from getting there, when I can do
it in my own way, which is to scull myself up, working
the old skiff up from bridge to bridge – Maidenhead to
Henley – from an early start on the Tuesday morning.
She will be waiting at Maidenhead in all her unadorned
beauty – that is, without an ounce of the unnecessary
weighty lumber, gratings, carpets, the board up forrard,
the cushions and rail, that among them make pretty
nearly one man's work to tug along. Why ever on earth
people want to clutter up a boat and weigh her down
with a cargo of lumber I never can make out. No more
pleasant journey than this is to be found on the Thames
if, that is, you time yourself right and are well under
way, so as to be able to dodge through the locks where
rollers are not without getting hung up by late flotillas –
punts, skiffs, and the like. Somehow, conducting rafts
of this sort seems to imbue the watermen or boatyard
persons in charge with crooked twists of temper and
surliness, such as used to characterize the typical turn-
pike man. The midsummer overfed Thames waterside
character very quickly becomes a cheeky, greedy, ex-
tortionate churl, during the short reign of fat times,
and fully justifies the biting sarcasm which represents

his kidney as making corners in lamb at midsummer and similar thrusts in sheep's heads when midwinter comes. Awkward fellow-travellers these are, delighted to make you lose a lock if they can. Exceptions there are, I expect, but I never found one.

Martin Cobbett, *Sporting Notions*, 1908

The setting matches the event. Sometimes it more than matches it :

Let the show be cheap or dear, it is to some of us one of *the* most enjoyable in the calendar of sport. You can get a lot of all-round pleasure out of it, more particularly if you sojourn in the neighbourhood pro tem. From Marsh Lock to Hambleden are reaches which for natural charms are hard, very hard, to beat. Henley itself is a pretty town, typical of that quarter of our island. Most of us have a sort of affection for the grey old bridge . . . picturesquely venerable. The church is an old friend, as was the Lion; also the Angel and the Catherine Wheel, not forgetting certain out-of-the-way pubs beloved of the well-informed, who do take much ease at these inns . . .

You can in regatta times get a very great deal of amusement for nothing in and about Henley, and, if you know how, may double your holiday by boating in ordinary fashion in the earlier hours of the forenoon when traffic on the river scarcely rises above normal proportions, and doing the regatta later as a separate course in the menu.

Regatta Reach is a charming one for the contemplative sportsman's morning paddle, when the crowd has not come out, but the waterside inhabitants, such as moorhens, water rats, dabchicks, and the rest have not gone frightened into hiding but are busying about. Haymaking is almost always in progress in regatta week, and never is the scent of the hay-fields drawn over your course more sweetly than down Fawley Court way early a-mornings. The cattle lead their placid lives as if no such word as hurry was in the vocabulary of the young, middle-aged, or old. On all evenings but one – Fridays – you may be at ease paddling in the gloaming, or as much later as you please.

Martin Cobbett, *Sporting Notions*, 1908

The rowing schools take great pride in sending crews to Henley. Rivalries last for generations. Theodore Cook first went to the Regatta in 1882 as a schoolboy at Radley, running along the tow-path and cheering his crew, who lost the final of the Ladies' Plate to Eton. In 1885 he was made Radley's Captain of Boats and rowed in seat no. 5 in the eight for the Ladies' Plate :

It is difficult to imagine that anyone ever could be happier than in that extraordinary combination of responsibility and enjoyment. We drove from Radley in a four-in-hand. Eton in a smarter coach than ours, met us on the very centre of the bridge. The two captains exchanged solemn salutes.

T. A. Cook, *The Sunlit Hours*, 1925

They never met on the water, Radley losing their heat to Corpus Christi and Eton going on to win the pot. If your school eight consider themselves superior to other mortals it ill behoves them to lose, as the crew from Shrewsbury once found out :

As for the school eight, they were gods or thought they were, except when they lost in the Princess Elizabeth Cup to Tiffin. At that stage Tiffin, subsequently recognized as a rowing force to be reckoned with, were almost unheard of. When the school went to first lesson next morning not a chair was in the classrooms. Under cover of darkness some 500 of them had been removed to the 1st XI cricket field where they were set out to spell in monster capitals, TIFFIN. It was a remarkable operation which, incidentally, the sternest inquest never solved. It was man's revenge, to bring the gods down a peg or eight. If they wanted to swagger in their special treatment they had better not lose like that.

Jeremy Alexander, *The Field*, 1981

A regatta sometimes gives relief from hard times, albeit with unusual measures to keep the enemy away:

In 1941 one day's racing was arranged at Henley for such schools as could manage the journey thither; eleven did. This provided a few glorious moments of relief in increasingly difficult times. The crew stayed away one night in Henley at Normanhurst where Mrs Powell their 'landlady' had, with some self-sacrifice, accumulated a store of food for them. On the water crews were to race four abreast from the Island to a little beyond the usual regatta finish: but the course presented a strange spectacle, for it was liberally dotted with posts driven into the river bed so that the straight stretch of water could not be used for landing planes – German not English. The crew, much under trained, acquitted itself well, though it suffered defeats which on paper look bad, though they were in fact very near misses for considerable success. The boat had been sent to Henley by rail; it is a comment on the times that the railway had insisted that its white canvas cover should be camouflaged. The labs did their best with permanganate which was the origin of the patchy pinky shades that the cover bore for many years well after the war was over. Boating took place from Leander Club.

R. D. Hole, *Monkton Combe School Boat Club*, 1978

Finding excuses for losing races is a common pastime, often shown up by a comparative study of accounts by partisans and official records – although, in fairness, official records often leave much out and much desired. Monkton Combe School met Pembroke College, Cambridge in the Ladies' Plate in 1920:

Monkton Combe v Pembroke, Cambridge, at Henley, 1920

A strong head wind, blowing down in gusts, was a decided check to the lighter crew, and would of necessity involve a bad time for the race. Pembroke was on the Berks side of the river which was likely to give them a slight advantage until the quarter-mile was passed, when the crew on the Bucks side would have, in their turn, an advantage. Monkton had a bad 'start' and Pembroke were up half a length, a lead which they afterwards increased to about two lengths. The Forleigh (*sic*) time was 3.59 mins. After this, Monkton rowed splendidly, and by means of frequent spurts, gradually decreased the lead of Pembroke. At the finish there was hardly daylight between the boats. Although there were faults in the crew, notably shortness in the water, it is a tribute to their training that they were practically the only school crew which did not fall to pieces towards the end of the course. Although the VIII were beaten, they acquitted themselves in a manner worthy of the highest traditions of Monkton rowing, and amply justified their entry for the Ladies' Plate. The Pembroke crew averaged a stone and a half heavier per man than the Monkton VIII. Later on in the day, under easier conditions, Pembroke beat Radley by three-quarters of a length.

The Monktonian, 1920

Pembroke led the whole way and won easily.

Henley Records, 1920

Rowing is a sport which gives its participants surprising satisfactions in the face of and in spite of defeat. In 1920 the Captain of Boats at Balliol College, Oxford, an Australian Rhodes Scholar called Hugh Cairns, invited his friend Rudyard Kipling to accompany the crew to Henley. Cairns took himself out of the boat to coach:

Mr Kipling was all attention, a stop watch concealed in his pocket, timing the crews who were rowing 'courses'. Since he could see starts from the Leander Club enclosure opposite the finishing post, he was able to time all our likely competition in the first two or three days. Nobody knew what he was doing. He was as furtive as a Newmarket clocker at early-morning gallops. He said the only other spy he detected was a bishop whose pink Leander cap clashed so violently with his purple bib that nobody in the enclosure could take their eyes off him. This chromatic disturbance fascinated Kipling. Greatly impressed with the influx of rowing clergy, he was convinced that a superb and stately crew composed entirely of bishops and deans, who were members of Leander, could be put on the river for a five-hundred-yard display.

After ten days at Henley, the Regatta opened with Balliol in fairly good shape. We won our first heat against the Royal Military College by a length, but in the draw for the second day, we had been told the bad news. We were to row against Eton on Thursday. Although Eton was a public school, its crew was almost always better than the average college. This year was no exception. We faced an eight that had been superbly trained and was a good five pounds per man heavier than we were. Mr Kipling had timed them over a trial course at seven minutes, seventeen seconds, exactly their time in the heat against us. They won by a length. It was a galling defeat. We were rowed out. I couldn't breathe and held my head down between my knees. As we drifted under Henley Bridge, I remember a kindly cockney voice calling, 'Good old three – don't worry, you'll live!'

We paddled back to the boathouse and carried *Lady Dervorguilla* to her rack. Hugh Cairns and Mr Kipling appeared. They had watched the race from the umpire's launch and looked far from dejected.

'You rowed well, the best form you've showed,' Hugh told us. 'Now take it easy and about half-past seven tonight I'm going to put you over the course again, against the clock.'

We relaxed until about seven o'clock that night, then we took the shining shell out and paddled up to Temple Island. There we did some starts and short bursts of rowing. One of the substitutes got in the starting punt and steadied us for a start. Hugh called from the bank: 'I'll start you with a gun ... COME FORWARD ... ARE YOU READY? ... THE SHOT!' We were off. Arengo Jones, our stroke, set us about forty the first minute and then he settled down to what seemed about thirty-five. Something astonishing had happened. The boat was moving forward without our effort. As we came forward, she seemed to slide ahead of us. It was an extraordinary sensation of smooth movement. I felt I was slacking but I dared not press for we were, for the first time, completely together in a rhythmic cycle. Arengo was giving us great length and maintaining the rate of stroke. From the bank, Hugh Cairns on his bike shouted, 'Oh, well rowed, Balliol!'

We were passing the 1500-yard post. I could hardly believe we had come that far. Kimber, the cox, cried, 'Give her ten, Balliol!' and counted us through, Jones bringing us up to forty. We were nearly at Phyllis Court now. We could hear an orchestra playing. It was so easy. Good Lord, there's the enclosure on the Bucks side. Again Kimber shouted, 'Now row her in, Balliol, give her ten!' Ten good long ones we gave her, and it was over. 'Easy all, Balliol!'

From the bank by the Leander enclosure, now empty in the dusk, came Hugh's delighted words, 'Well rowed, Balliol, oh, well rowed!' Mr Kipling was shouting the time, but we couldn't hear him. We paddled back to the boathouse and, as we lifted the *Lady Dervorguilla* over our heads and placed her on the rack, Hugh, Mr Kipling and the substitutes came into the boathouse. We heard the good news that our time had been seven minutes and ten seconds – three seconds better than Eton's in the morning. It was the best row I ever had, practically in the dark, racing against the clock, with no one to see us except Hugh Cairns and Rudyard Kipling.

Raymond Massey, from *My Oxford*, 1977

Marlow

Foul Play

In the case of skiffs fouling, all jostling is allowable which can be accomplished with the sculls in the row-locks, and the rower on his seat.

Durham Regatta regulations, 1837

On the whole rowing is a clean sport. On modern straight buoyed courses there is little opportunity for fouling, but there are more opportunities in two-crew river races for doubtful steering and 'washing' opponents, i.e. manœuvring in such a way that they take the brunt of one's wake. Psychology can come into play as well, like keeping one's opponents waiting at the start, or trying to get off with a slight advantage.No regatta today would tolerate the rules from Durham. In Durham things certainly got out of hand sometimes, particularly in 1860 :

In the Scurry Stakes there were five entries – M. Craggs in 'Little Agnes', G. D. Newby in 'Phantom', J. H. Clasper in 'Tat', T. Robinson in 'Never Despair', and J. Bone in 'Isis'. The cutters were to start from Count's Corner and row through Elvet Bridge and back. 'On the firing of the pistol for the start a very exciting scene took place. It appears that several of the competitors entertained a bad feeling towards Clasper because they considered that he, being one of the best rowers of the day, should not have entered to deprive an amateur of the prize; therefore they determined at any cost to deprive him of it. On the boats starting Robinson endeavoured to pull right into Clasper's boat, but missing it the oars became entangled, when the former jumped out of his boat and tried to pull the latter out of his. Clasper, seeing that all chance of winning the race was gone, and that his boat was likely to be capsized in the struggle, hit Robinson on the head with his fist, and was just on the point of striking him with his oar when he found that his boat was fast filling with water and going down bow foremost, and to save himself he had to jump out and swim to shore. On arriving at Bow Corner, Bone placed his boat right across the river, for the purpose of fouling Newby. Succeeding in his object both boats became entangled and immediately afterwards Newby's boat upset and, in tumbling out, its occupant seized hold of Bone's boat and upset it. Both parties after a good ducking succeeded in reaching the shore. The race was ultimately won by Craggs.'

It might have been supposed that this was enough unseemly behaviour for one day, but the hostility to the Claspers extended to the Patron's Plate. The first heat in this race was between the Claspers and Newby's crew and was claimed by the latter on a foul which was decided against them by the stewards. This enraged the Durham populace and the final heat between the Claspers and the Taylors could not take place 'in consequence of some foolish and ill-judged Durham men pelting the Claspers with stones from the banks, and preventing them going up to the starting point. The greatest race of the Regatta was thus prevented coming off and the spectators lost the opportunity of seeing some most splendid rowing. The stewards determined to divide the prize between the Taylors and the Claspers. Newby expressed to the stewards his regret that any interruption should have prevented the race, but of course he could not prevent the foolish conduct of his friends.'

There were three entries for the Wear Scurry:– W. Brignall in 'Amrith', J. Farmer in 'Up to the Scratch', and H. S. Whatley in the 'Divine'. 'An exciting fouling battle took place on starting between Brignall and Farmer. The former made several attempts to row over his opponent's boat. In the scuffle Farmer lost an oar and was compelled to give in. Brignall then pursued Whatley and on his overtaking him a foul took place, and Whatley's boat capsized, Brignall being also thrown out of his boat into which, however, he contrived again to get, and to reach the winning post first. As all three competitors fouled with the hand, against the regulations, the stewards adjudged the prize to Brignall as having got to the winning post first.'

In the University Plate, University College beat the School after a level race to Baths' Bridge, there being no further entries. The Stewards' Plate was won by 'St Cuthbert' (Univ. Coll. II.), after beating the School, who fouled the arch of Elvet Bridge, and Hatfield Hall, who had beaten the Wear B. C. in the first round.

Capt. A. A. Macfarlane-Grieve, *A History of Durham Rowing*,
1922

Certainly professional rowing was more prone to fouling than amateur because of the big money prizes on offer and the huge market in side bets. Wise was the competitor who

*kept a guard on his boat the night before the challenge,
ensuring that the rudder or the fin on the bottom was not
loosened, that the outriggers and rowlocks were not inter-
fered with, that the leather 'button' on the oar or scull which
fits into the rowlock was not readjusted. A few millimetres
can make all the difference to one's form. Then there were
bribed stake-boat boys, bad or blind judges, and untrust-
worthy foreigners, like at the great international regatta
on the Seine near Paris in 1867 :*

It had been hoped that the New Brunswickers would
have tried their mettle against our watermen, and thus
given a fair opportunity of judging of the relative merits
of their boats and style of rowing, but they scornfully
kept aloof, calling the Seine a mere 'mud-creek', and
offering to make a match on the St Lawrence or one of
our own estuaries. Tagg, Caffin, and Clasper each
brought a crew to the post, and were met by some
watermen from Amsterdam, who were conspicuous in
bright blue jackets. At the start, the English watermen,
as usual, stole a lead – cheating the Amsterdam boat of
a clear length. The starter, however, allowed the race
to continue. Past the stand the order was Tagg, Caffin,
Amsterdam, Clasper, and in this order they continued
till near the finish, when the Amsterdam crew spurted
very rapidly, and appeared just to pass their adversaries.
The judge, however, placed them third, to their very
great disappointment. . . . Thus ended the great Paris
regatta. If we look at the quality of the rowing and the
fame of the oarsmen we cannot but regard it as a magnificent success; if at the number of spectators and the
interest generally excited, as a not less complete failure.
This failure has beyond doubt been partly due to the
exclusive and unconciliatory character which English-
men unhappily not unfrequently display . . .

C. P. Scott, *Manchester Guardian*, 1867

If we divn't behave weel tiv him, ye see,
His ghost, when he's deed, 'ill be seen frae the kee
In a skill 'side the bridge 'bout twelve iviry neet,
Till the mornin' cock craws, then he'll row oot
    iv seet.
        Spirited Harry, the pride iv wor river,
        Yor name it will flourish when ye're gyen
           for iver.

          John Taylor, 'On Harry Clasper', 1860s

The Thames may have more rowing than anywhere else, but it certainly does not hold a monopoly. The Tyne was a great rival during the days of the English and World Professional Sculling Championships. Geordies watched rowing in their hundreds of thousands. Their famous champions had grand funerals and large monuments, and the best songwriters of the day hymned their feats and their tragedies, as John Taylor did for Harry Clasper in 1860, above, and as Geordie Ridley reported back on Bob Chambers's defeat of the Australian R. A. W. Green from Putney to Mortlake in 1863:

    Now lads, ye've heerd of Chambers,
    He's bet the Asstrilyen Green,
    For pulling a skiff there is ne doot
    He's the best ther's ivor been.
    He has regular locomotiv speed,
    He's upreet, honest and true
    Wheniver he pulls wiv a pair ov sculls
    Aw puts on ivory screw!

Now when Bob and Green they pulled
    thor match
This Green luik'd very wild,
He tuik the lead of Bob at forst
Till they got abyun a mile.
But Harry gov Bob the office then,
Saying aw'l lay ten to ite,
The reporter of the Chronicle said
That Greeny then turned white.

Geordie Ridley

The gospels of rowing spread to wherever there was suitable water, and to all parts of the globe, especially the English-speaking parts. Soldiers raced ships' boats when becalmed on troop-carriers in the Indian Ocean; the engineers of the Canadian Pacific took their sport from the St Lawrence at Montreal to the Pacific at Vancouver, building a club at the end of the line; a bishop from St John's College, Cambridge took rowing to his see of New Zealand; the bankers took it to Shanghai and the generals to the Hooghly in India. Londoners established it on the Volga, ships' crews raced on the Hudson, the Europeans opened clubs in South America. The coastal towns of Britain, the rivers of England and Ireland, and even the Irwell and

the *Bridgewater Canal boast rowing clubs. From here we'll take a whistle stop paddle to a few nooks and outposts of rowing's far-flung empire, starting with a song which has inspired many unprintable versions but which was written by a housemaster to the glory of his sport and school. The music for the 'Eton Boating Song' was composed by old boys in their regimental mess in the Punjab:*

Jolly boating weather,
    And a hay harvest breeze,
Blade on the feather,
    Shade off the trees,
Swing, swing together
    With your bodies between your knees.

Skirting past the rushes,
    Ruffling o'er the weeds,
Where the lock-stream gushes,
    Where the cygnet feeds,
We'll see how the wine-glass flushes
    At supper on Boveney meads.

Dreadnought, Britannia, Thetis,
    St George, Prince of Wales, and *Ten*
And the eight poor souls whose meat is
    Hard steak and a harder hen,
And the end of our long boat fleet is
    Defiance to Westminster men.

Harrow may be more clever,
    Rugby may make more row,
But we'll row for ever
    Steady from stroke to bow,
And nothing in life shall sever
    The chain that is round us now.

Others will fill our places
   Dressed in the old light blue;
We'll recollect our races,
   We'll to the flag be true,
And youth will be still in our faces
   When we cheer for an Eton crew.

Twenty years hence this weather
   May tempt us from office stools,
We may be slow on the feather
   And seem to the boys old fools,
But we'll still swing together
   And swear by the best of schools.

William Cory 1863

Horace Walpole went to Richmond-on-Thames regatta in
1791 :

On Monday was the boat-race. I was in the great room
at the Castle, with the Duke of Clarence, Lady Di.,
Lord Robert Spencer, and the House of Bouverie, to
see the boats start from the bridge to Thistleworth, and
back to a tent erected on Lord Dysart's meadow, just
before Lady Di.'s windows; whither we went to see
them arrive, and where we had breakfast. For the
second heat, I sat in my coach on the bridge; and did
not stay for the third. The day had been coined on
purpose, with my favourite south-east wind. The
scene, both up the river and down, was what only
Richmond upon earth can exhibit. The crowds on
those green velvet meadows and on the shores, the
yachts, barges, pleasure and small boats, and the
windows and gardens lined with spectators, were so
delightful, that when I came home from that vivid
show, I thought Strawberry looked as dull and solitary
as a hermitage . . .

Horace Walpole, *Richmond Boat Race*, 1791

On Boxing Day in 1927 Bert Barry, watched by his brother Lou who was wearing a 'maroon golfing suit', beat Major Goodsell of Australia for the world professional sculling title on the freezing Fraser River in Vancouver, British Columbia. Goodsell - Major was his given name - had beaten Barry on Labour Day earlier that year, and the Vancouver Sun *reported the return match :*

Through a broad avenue of fir-clad hills, their slopes slowly dipping, it seemed, in belated acknowledgement of his undoubted prowess, Bert Barry, phlegmatic Englishman, rowed Major Goodsell of Australia into submission within five minutes of the get-away. A new world champion was hailed twenty-one minutes and four seconds after the start.

Barry's triumph was as convincing as his defeat was crushing to his friends last September. The day was rather like that of their first meeting when Goodsell was never headed, and rowed away as he pleased.

There was no tumultuous cheering, however, yesterday, and there were no thousands lining the southern slope of the inlet, nor dashing frantically along the bank in pursuit of the oarsmen. Barry commanded the situation every foot of the three-mile distance.

From the bows of the *Harbour Princess* came the cold voice of Umpire George Pocock, occasionally warning too enthusiastic adherents of Goodsell to cease signalling. [Barry's brother Lou's] excitement was evidently in contrast with that of his elder brother, who took his victory as modestly as he had carried on ever since he arrived in Canada.

Vancouver Sun, 27 December 1927

Rowing was particularly dangerous in Shanghai between August and November 1937 :

Scull down-river on Thursday evening to inspect Japanese 'Armada' of some 40 ships – much activity of naval launches and vigorous display of signalling – average age of warships something high – tiffin-time [a light lunch] finds Club packed with Shanghai Scottish Co. – Club members in mere civilian garb find difficulty in securing Boys' attention for service – audible gunfire on Friday 13th afternoon – George comes early on Saturday morning to complain Bath not filled with fresh water for Swimming Gala—assure him that there will be no Gala, bomb dropped on Hongkew Wharf shortly afterwards lends colour to this assumption – events of the afternoon cause day to be known as 'Bloody Saturday'.

Artillery duel on Monday night between Chinese batteries in Pootung and Japanese warships gives little rest to Shanghai Scottish – shells whistle by and some drop in Creek near Club – torpedo aimed at veteran *Idzumo* hits wharf nearby and shakes Club; Corporal Neil sleeping on bed near Bath awakes with start and falls in water – evacuation of Shanghai Scottish to more 'desirable residence'.

Club then closed – Boats carried by Coolies to Cricket Club for safety, during wee small hours with police escort – severe shock for any wandering pedestrian (with curfew pass) to meet Eight upside down, proceeding like a giant caterpillar down Nanking Road – sole occupant of Club the Number One Laodah – questioned, replied 'S'pose I go, who man looksee?' – Demise of the Club motorboat *Woody*, which was under-going repairs over at Pootung when hostilities began, and became innocent victim of concentrated gunfire.

Club re-opened on 1st September – first tiffin a fiasco, since food left in ice box since middle August was causing lid to jump up and down – Boys nearly dropping plates and Club-house shaking when *Idzumo* fired broadsides – Battle started when Destroyer opened fire on a sampan woman yulohing up river – said woman continued to yuloh imperturbably to safety, and Chinese trench mortars took up the tale – from Club roof excellent view of shells dropping in river some 300 yards away – two shrapnel bursts hit Japanese Consulate opposite – Committee meeting at Club that evening decided Club Opening premature – argument reinforced by stray shells and bullets whizzing down Soochow Road – Club closed again on 4th September.

Swiss member killed in bombing episode near Wing On department store.

Club opened once more on 28th September – rowing on the deserted Creek permitted 'at members' own risk' – Bow of the first Four out decided 'Prevention better than Cure' and wore his Tin Hat – 'Eyes in the boat' excellent maxim, but good view not to be missed of Japanese Bombers 'laying eggs' on North Station half a mile away – Trench Mortar explosions caused 'Time' to falter occasionally – Club building unscathed except for one bullet hole through Boathouse window

– return of Club Fleet from Race Course in stages –
ingenious wooden frame fixed over Committee member's car carried all boats back at nocturnal trysts.

N. M. W. Harris, *Sampan Pidgin*, 1938

*You could have too much of a good thing in China even
before the Sino-Japanese conflict. Sport often gets in the
way of pleasure, illustrated by E. Kraps's portrait of
E. T. Byrne of the Shanghai Club early this century – 'à
la Mandalay,' wrote Kraps, 'with apologies to R. Kipling' :*

By the ancient lower Boathouse, looking north-
　　ward on the Creek,
There is someone there a-swearin'; it's a treat
　　to 'ear 'im speak;
For the wind blows through 'is sweater, and
　　the little waves they say;
'Stay at Home you British rower, for you
　　can't go out to-day!'

　　No! we won't go out to-day
　　Where the river steamers lay;
　　Can't you see the chow-chow water is
　　　　too strong for you to-day?
　　No! you can't go out to-day,
　　Where the sampan coolies play,
　　An' the smells come up like poison outer
　　　　'ongkew' crost the way!

'Is rowing togs is yaller an' 'is speech a little
　　blue,
An 'is name is Secretary an' 'e runs the
　　British crew,
An' I seed 'im first a-smokin' of a stinkin'
　　bad cigar,
An' a-wastin' Christian cusses on an 'eathen
　　coolie's ma;

Bloomin' Chinese 'ooker's son –
Wot they called the number one –
Plucky lot 'e cared for coolies when I
    cussed 'im till 'e run!
No! you can't go out to-day . . .

When them German beggars come out an'
    started for to row,
'E'd git 'is useless carcase 'id an' 'oller out
    'what 'O!'
'E thought they could'nt work it but upon my
    sinful soul,
They yanked 'er thro' the Garden Bridge
    without a bloomin' roll.

Not a sanguinary roll
Right acrost the Garden shoal
They swung along that even that 'e
    scratched 'is ruddy poll!
No! you can't go out to-day . . .

But that's all shove behind me – long ago an'
    fur away,
An' there ain't no eight-oars runnin' from
    the Club to Sicawei;
    An' I'm learnin' 'ere in Shang'ai what the
    ten-year oarsman tells;
If you've 'eard the Bar a-callin', you won't
    never 'eed naught else;

No! you won't 'eed nothin' else
But them spicy cocktail smells,
The bamboo an' the gin-tail an' the
    whiskey in the spells;
No! you can't go out to-day . . .

I am sick o' wastin' cusses on a shapeless
  griffins' four.
An' the blassted scullin' races do not hinterest
  no more
Tho' I drinks with old busters that rowed
  twelve years ago,
An' they talks a lot o' rowin', but lor'! wot do
  they know?

> What the dickens do they know?
> Much too old an' fat to row,
> I've a kinder, sorter notion that they do
>   it all for show!
> But we won't go out to-day . . .

Ship me somewhere's north of Frenchtown,
  where the best is 'No. 2'
Where there ain't no bloomin' trainin' an' I'm
  as good as you;
For the poppin' corks are callin', an' it's there
  that I would be –
By the old Chung Way Bar sober, just
  a-startin' on a spree;

> Not much! we won't go out to-day,
> Where the river steamers lay;
> Be damned to the chow-chow water and
>   have a drink to-day!
> No! you can't go out to-day,
> Where the sampan coolies play
> An' the smells come up like poison
>   outer' ongkew' crost the way.

E. Kraps (C. E. Sparke), 'Not Today'

An Irish function always cheers the soul:

Sunday was local regatta day on Inniscarra, celebrating
Shandon Boat Club's one hundred and first year. The

programme described the amazing history of Cork rowing, e.g., 'The greatest number of oarsmen ever seen at one regatta met at Cork in 1902 to compete for the International Trophy and other prizes which the Leander Club successfully defended against Berlin Rowing Club.' Buses and boat trailers were stuck in farm lanes, and for the morning your man on the loud-speaker talked entirely to himself since no spectators braved his enclosure, preferring the boat park side where the loudspeaker was often turned off.

In the afternoon things hotted up. An English girls crew won a race and were disqualified because they carried a boy as cox, banned under the Irish rules. A boat appeared called Stroke Me Gently . . . Your man announced: 'An important announcement. A sum of money was found at the disco in Coachford last evening. We have good reason to believe it belongs to a female person and if the owner will present herself to me we can make a financial arrangement.' An Irishman said his hotel breakfast was lousy: 'A shrivelled rasher and a parrot's egg.' The farmers sat on the water's edge watching the races while listening on transistors to the Cork versus Kerry Gaelic football final replay in extra time, at which the rest of Ireland was in attendance. The English team formed two composite crews of men and ladies – as the Irish insist on calling them – who never managed to meet at the start. Commentaries from the Montreal Olympics were switched into your man's public address system, revealing Sean Drea's near miss at a medal in the single sculls. Several team managers and oarsmen tested the waters of Inniscarra. Your man announced: 'The sum of money has now been restored to the loser and she has now become a winner,' England won the Home Countries International Rowing Match and Ireland won the day.

Christopher Dodd, *The Guardian*, 1976

. . . and more of Cork, scene of an international regatta
arranged by Lord Chief Justice O'Brien in 1902 :

Leander came
Wid their roll of fame
But Henley had made them look crazy now
Wid their caps of pink
They could make you blink
And their cox saying 'Arrah, be aisy now.'
They were cheerful and gay
In their English way
And they never looked to be troublin', boys,
Till they caught a sight
Of the black and white
Of the Trinity College, Dublin, boys.

The Ruderverein
Looked mighty fine,
And, oh, but its confident still I am
That they'll make us blow
When they start to row
These lads of the Emperor William.
They smoked no pipes
But they drank their swipes
And they ate their mutton and chicken up,
And donner and blitz,
They gave us fits
Wid their German moustaches stickin' up!

Emmanuel too
Looked neat and new
From the banks of the Cam, where the willows
are,
They had travelled to see
The River Lee
Where the currents and tides and the billows
are.

There were Oxford blues
  In their College crews
And they didn't mean to be dawdlin' there,
  In the head of the Isis,
  Dressed up nice
And the scarlet College of Magdalen there.

From the South and the North
  Of the Isle came forth,
The Irishmen, full of devilry,
  They were broths of boys
  For the fun and noise,
And good at rowing and revelry.
  And when they had done
  There was one crew won,
And eight of the rowers were frisky there,
  But none of the rest
  Looked much depressed
For they knew there was plenty of whiskey
    there!

'TIS.', *Punch*, 1902

*Souvenir hunting breaks out from time to time. In 1912
Sydney RC of Australia beat England's Leander in the
Grand Challenge Cup at Henley with George V and Queen
Mary watching from the umpire's launch. Then Leander
beat Sydney in the Olympic semi-final in Stockholm:*

[100]

On their return, many of the oarsmen ascribed their loss in the Olympics to their lane, Leander having 'well over a length's advantage'. According to Middleton [one of the crew], they could beat Leander nine times out of ten on a straight course. English rowing generally, he said, 'taught us little or nothing' regarding rowing or the fitting of racing boats. The accusation was also made that Leander failed to congratulate the Australians after the Henley success. These comments earned Middleton an English press description as 'petulant and lacking in sportsmanship', while Horniman [an Australian official] caused a stir by announcing that Middleton would be 'most severely censured' for his 'rude comments'. A motion of disapproval was, however, later defeated. Although the boat was sold to Thames Rowing Club after its Henley win, the stroke and bow seats were brought back by E. S. Marks, President of the NSW Sports Club, and were suitably mounted. The oars used at Henley were also brought back to Australia and were presented to the crew (while the flag from the Royal Barge also, mysteriously, found its way back to Australia).

A. L. May, *Sydney Rows*, 1970

Extravagant claims are wont to be made for the educational influences of good oarsmen :

Charles Hose went down before his due time to enter the civil service in Sarawak, where he carried out valuable scientific researches in his leisure hours. His most striking achievement, however, was that he induced the pagans of Borneo to give up head-hunting as a method of settling tribal disputes and take to boat-racing instead.

F. Brittain, *A Short History of Jesus College, Cambridge*, 1940

Clubs and crews evolve their own customs and folk lore.
In Durham the evils of smoking were not always heeded:

Four tired but jubilant watermen (more or less) return
from their labours; tea is waiting in somebody's room;
and now for the first smoke.

The first smoke was a solemn affair, not to be lightly
approached, and many were the devices used to secure
the best effects. One man always had a cigarette in his
mouth before he was actually out of the boat, and
handed over his rigger to somebody else while he lit up:
a long draw, a mighty inhale, and smoke could almost
be seen oozing out of his shins. Another – a determined
fellow this – adopted a very peculiar proceeding: – with
the object of breaking himself of smoking altogether,
on the last night before training began, he would smoke
half way through a pipe, and then carefully put it by till
training was over; his first smoke was the old half pipe,
which, theoretically, would be his last; but not a bit of
it! The pipe tasted like ambrosia, and smelt – to him –
like attar-of-roses: the only people who were in favour
of his giving up smoking were the other people in the
room at the time.

In various ways the ritual of the First Smoke is
performed; much tea is drunk and cake consumed; a
bath, a hurried dressing, and we are ready for the prizes.

Revd D. H. S. Mould in *A History of Durham Rowing*, 1922

In Chester they are a little smug about spiritual welfare:

The Rev J. Folliott was appointed Chaplain to the
Club in 1843. The office has since been found unnecessary.

The Royal Chester Rowing Club Centenary History 1838–1938, 1939

In Dublin matrimony was penalized:

The early records [of the Pembroke Club, Dublin]

[102]

contain very little about the actual rowing activities of the members and the entries are largely in respect of the business transacted at the various meetings of the club; the adoption of rules, improvement of premises, etc. One item recording a resolution passed in 1840 is interesting and reads as follows:-

'Resolved that any member marrying shall forfeit a dozen of champagne to the club which shall be drunk by the members of the club at such time and place as shall be agreed upon by them.'

T. F. Hall, *History of Boat Racing in Ireland,* 1937

At Monkton Combe cattle had to be admitted as members :

The fact that farmers have rights of passage across the frontage of the boat-houses has been the cause of much discomfort. . . . Many will recollect how young heifers crowded under the floor of the old wooden boat-house in hot weather, seldom failing to leave abundant evidence of their presence.

R. D. Hole, *Monkton Combe School Boat Club,* 1978

Everywhere the annual dinner or dance has to be arranged. The professionals have left the Tyne but the amateurs thrive there, though perhaps with less style than they did in the 1930s. The minutes of Tyne Amateur RC's Dance Committee document a series of meetings which took place throughout 1938 and into the next year. The surviving min-ute book starts in 1937. None of the reports give much clue about the business conducted but they are an excellent guide to the quality of brew and public houses of that city :

The 27th meeting of the Dance Committee was ap-parently held in the Cannon Inn, Billy Mill, on Sunday 24 October 1937. The Secretary was not present. No minutes were read. Mr Walker appears to have been elected Hon. Treasurer of the Dance, having unselfishly volunteered to perform the onerous duties of this office.

Reports on this gin palace and the beer retailed there are on the whole favourable. The Secretary learns that the black ball awarded him for his absence was later discharged from the Cannon by Mr Brown. No knowledge of its further whereabouts has come to hand.

The 38th and last minuted meeting started in the Crow's Nest, Haymarket, on Wednesday 1 February 1939:

Messrs Anderson and Newcombe did not attend. No minutes were read; there were no minutes to read.

Mr Walker announced that the Dance had made an actual profit.

A hearty vote of thanks was extended by the Committee to Mr Walker for his wizardry with the Dance finances.

The downstairs buffet at this house has recently been redecorated with more than ordinary care, and the beer (Newcastle Breweries) was palatable, if nothing else.

This meeting having been called in part to celebrate the approaching nuptials of Mr Walton, members were gratified to learn that the Chairman had with him a book of no little interest to those about to enter the marital state. Perusal of this volume, the sentiments and diagrams therein, proved both instructive and entertaining; and the evening's jollification was rounded off with a visit to the Palace Theatre, where the pantomime 'Jack and the Beanstalk' was still playing to empty houses. The advent of the Committee considerably livened up the show, and it was gratifying to learn that the Giant was evidently intimate with the family affairs of at least one member.

A bag of nuts was offered to the band, but they refused to play.

Brian A. Brown, *Tyne ARC Dance Committee Minutes*, 1939

The Oarsman's Farewell to his Oar

Farewell, dear companion of labour and pastime,
  My hands shall encircle your handle no more.
This day on the Thames we were joined for the
      last time;
  Our last racing stroke has been rowed, oh my
      oar.
And thus of the story that bound us together,
  That made you my servant and kept you my
      friend
'Mid the chances and changes of temper and
      weather,
  The last word is spoken, and now comes the end.

Many oars have I had – lo! these cups are a
      token –
  Since first a raw Freshman I splashed in a crew;
Their shafts may be warped and their blades may
      be broken,
  But their staunchness lived on to be centred in
      you.
Lo! all these old oars that I lost with or won with
  Return to remind me of failure or fame.
The traditions are yours of those blades I have
      done with;
  The wood may have changed, but the soul is the
      same.

Great days of rejoicing and strength and endeavour,
    When the blood galloped swift, and the muscles
        were taut,
So brightly they shone, that are vanished for ever,
    My heart from their radiance a glamour has
        caught.
And still, though the grey in my hair be
        increasing,
    Though the joints may be stiffened, the sinews
        unstrung,
The brightness is round me, and still without
        ceasing
    I think and remember and dream and am
        young.

                    R. C. Lehmann, *Anni Fugaces*, 1901

. . . and a final thought from Steve Fairbairn:

The dreamier a crew looks, the nearer it approaches to
the poetry of motion.

Acknowledgements

The editor and publishers gratefully acknowledge permission to use copyright material in this book:

Jeremy Alexander: from an article in *The Field*, 1981. Reprinted by permission of the author.

Max Beerbohm: from *Zuleika Dobson*. Copyright (1911; by Dodd, Mead & Co., Copyright renewed 1938 by Max Beerbohm. N/e Heinemann 1964/Dodd Mead 1978. Reprinted by permission of Wm. Heinemann Ltd., and Dodd, Mead & Co., Inc.

F. Brittain: from *A Short History of Jesus College* (W. Heffer & Sons Ltd., 1940). Reprinted by permission of Heffers Booksellers.

Anne Clark: from *The Real Alice* (1981). Reprinted by permission of Michael Joseph Ltd.

Steve Fairbairn: from *Slowly Forward*, edited F. Brittain (Kaye & Ward, 1951).

Vernard Foley & Werner Soedel: from an article entitled 'Ancient Oared Warships' from *Scientific American*, April 1981. Copyright © 1981 by Scientific American, Inc. All rights reserved. Reprinted by permission of W. H. Freeman & Co., Publisher.

F. T. Hall: from *History of Boat Racing in Ireland* (1937). Reprinted by permission of the Irish Amateur Rowing Union.

R. D. Hole: from *Monkton Combe School Boat Club*, 1978. Reprinted by permission of the author, and the Headmaster, R. A. C. Meredith.

Rudyard Kipling: 'Song of the Galley-Slaves' from *The Finest Story in the World*, first published in *Many Inventions* (Macmillan, London 1893). Reprinted by permission of A. P. Watt Ltd., for The National Trust and Macmillan London Limited.

J. W. Langfield and B. Grainger: extract slightly adapted from *Rudern* (German Democratic Republic textbook of rowing, by Dr Ernst Herberger *et al*), translated by J. W. Langfield and B. Grainger, 1974. Reprinted by permission.

John Masefield: extract from 'Cargoes' from *Poems* (Heinemann, r/e 1946/Macmillan New York, 1953). Originally published in *Ballads and Poems*, 1910. Reprinted by permission of The Society of Authors as the literary representative of the Estate of John Masefield, and of Macmillan Publishing Co., Inc.

ACKNOWLEDGEMENTS

Raymond Massey: from *My Oxford* (ed. Ann Thwaite, 1977). Reprinted by permission of Robson Books.

Henry Newbolt: extract from 'He Fell Among Thieves', in *Selected Poems of Henry Newbolt* (Hodder & Stoughton, 1981). Reprinted by permission of Peter Newbolt.

Ray Perrott: from an article entitled 'Tiers for Victory' which appeared in the *Sunday Times*, 26 April 1981. Reprinted by permission of Times Newspapers Ltd.

Sir Arthur Quiller-Couch: 'Alma Mater', first published in *Oxford Magazine*, 1896. Reprinted by permission of Monro Pennefather & Co.

While every effort has been made to secure permission we may have failed in a few cases to trace the copyright holder. We apologize for any apparent negligence.

The illustrations in this book were taken from W. B. Woodgate, *Boating* (London, 1889), and from *Punch*.

Index